the flight
and the
nest

the flight and the nest

CAROL LYNN PEARSON

BOOKCRAFT, INC.
Salt Lake City, Utah

Library of Congress Catalog Card Number: 75-31079
ISBN 0-88494-288-0

2nd Printing, 1976

LITHOGRAPHED IN U.S.A. BY
PUBLISHERS PRESS
SALT LAKE CITY, UTAH

On Nest Building

Mud is not bad for nest building.
Mud and sticks
And a fallen feather or two will do
And require no reaching.
I could rest there, with my tiny ones,
Sound for the season, at least.

But —
If I may fly awhile —
If I may cut through a sunset going out
And a rainbow coming back,
Color upon color sealed in my eyes —
If I may have the unboundaried skies
For my study,
Clouds, cities, rivers for my rooms —
If I may search the centuries
For melody and meaning —
If I may try for the sun —

I shall come back
Bearing such beauties
Gleaned from God's and man's very best.
I shall come filled.

And then —
Oh, the nest that I can build!

Contents

Illustrations

Preface

Ever since junior high school I had tried to figure out some very important and puzzling things concerning women — their history, their status, their relationship to the world in general. I had listened to the voices of many women speaking from many points of view. I had tried to make sense out of the extremes from which it seems the loudest voices usually come.

But a couple of years ago I made a wonderful discovery — sort of like finding buried treasure — in the basement of the old family home up in Dingle Dell, Idaho. Aunt Mamie and I had driven up with the express purpose of introducing me to some other voices, which she vaguely remembered, and which I had never heard: the voices of the women of my own heritage.

I had always known that if I ever met the women of the Mormon pioneer past, they could teach me a great deal — quilting, soap making, giving birth on the prairie, singing through incredible hardships, having faith in God and seeing that faith rewarded. But I never knew that they could teach me about some of the more sensitive issues of womanhood. I had forgotten that they lived during the age of woman's "emancipation." It never occurred to me that they had already done battle with many of the questions that are pertinent today and that I might learn from their observations and experiences. And I had no idea that (most wonderful of all) they had *written* — with strength and balance and good sense — about their journeys into this other frontier on which they and other women were unquestionably pioneers.

Reverence is not an inaccurate word to express what I felt when Aunt Mamie placed in my hands that first volume of the *Woman's Exponent* of 1880, wrapped in an old white curtain. (It qualified as a volume because the full year's issues had been carefully sewn together in a muslin binding.) Then followed box after box of other *Exponents,* and copies of the other two publications by and for Mormon women of many decades ago — the *Young Woman's Journal,* and the *Relief Society Magazine.* These had been carefully preserved by the subscribers, the women of my family, and bore their names at the top. Some were addressed to Mary Oakey, who left a comfortable home in Nottingham, England, when she and her husband, James, were baptized into The Church of Jesus Christ of Latter-day Saints and traveled to Utah, later being called to settle in Dingle Dell, not far from Bear Lake. Other of the publications were addressed to Sarah Oakey Sirrine, Mary's daughter, who had left all her dolls in England (a favorite family story) and had walked across the plains at the age of eight. Later issues bore the name of Emeline Sirrine, Sarah's daughter and my own mother, who died when I was fifteen. (She was named — and why not — for Emmeline B. Wells, who for more than forty years served as editor of the *Woman's Exponent.*)

I like to believe they were thinking of me when they boxed up rather than burned these old publications. Could they know that in later years I and uncounted others of my generation would be looking back in search of our roots? Could they know that the hearts of the daughters would be turned to the mothers, hungry to know them and to learn from them?

Into the trunk and the back seat went the printed voices of these women, and over the next many months they spoke to me as I read hundreds upon hundreds of these newspapers and magazines. Articles on many, many subjects, historical and inspirational, were there. But I especially searched for, and found, for it was one of the heaviest continuing themes to which they addressed themselves, their comments on the "woman question."

I make no pretense that this book is a thorough representation of what all the women did and felt, but I feel it is an accurate picture of the general feelings that were expressed by those who published and contributed to the periodicals. For complete biographical information on the women represented here, or for thorough treatment of their activities, the reader must go elsewhere. Many people are doing research into this general area, and their findings certainly deserve a good readership.

Nor do I suggest that all of the answers were found by these women and are here presented. Many of the issues they faced are very similar to those we face, and evidently are the same that will continue to be faced by women in years to come. Each generation must view the issues from a point of view that recognizes the peculiar circumstances of its own day. And each individual woman must find her own path, guided by the light of revealed truths, the light that is within her, and any light that others might shed.

For my own self, I have found considerable light radiating from those great women whose lives and writings constitute my own heritage. That others also might find them illuminating, I must share them.

CHAPTER 1

Only a Girl

In August 1872, a Mormon woman, scanning the pages of her newly arrived *Woman's Exponent* (this was only the fifth issue, and the LDS women were delighted to have their very own newspaper for women, one of the few in the nation), would have read the following account:

> A gentleman, recently married in Chicago, presented his bride at the wedding with the original transcript of one of the first dispatches ever sent over the first telegraph line, from Baltimore to Washington. It was the announcement to the lady's grandmother of her birth, and read, "Only a girl."[1]

The reader would likely have smiled, then sighed and shook her head. How true — how sadly true, this accumulation of centuries of tradition and superstition and darkness that had dictated the generally accepted notion that to come to earth as a girl child was not quite so desirable a thing as to come as a boy child.

If the reader had happened to be Susa Young, sixteen-year-old daughter of Brigham Young and Lucy Bigelow Young, she doubtless would have recalled, as she later wrote, that her mother, upon finding out Susa's sex, "exclaimed with great force, if not elegance, 'Shucks!' "[2]

---

[1] *Woman's Exponent,* 1 (August 1, 1872), 38.
[2] "The Editor Presumes to Talk About Herself," *Young Woman's Journal,* 7 (January 1896), 200.

Only a girl. So it had been, except for isolated periods, throughout the whole of history. But in these modern times — the last half of the nineteenth century — women were asking a question voiced only by radicals in times past. Why? Why *only?*

Attending the birth of Susa Young as "presiding high priestess of the occasion" was her Aunt Zina Huntington Young, who responded to the mother's disappointment, "No, it isn't all shucks, it's wheat, and full weight too."[3]

Susa went on, in her seventy-seven years, to demonstrate that she was indeed "full weight" — nothing "only" about her, as she took her place as a respected wife and mother of thirteen children, as well as one of the noted women of her day, accomplished as a writer, lecturer, genealogist, and reformer. The question of woman's position remained always in the foreground of her mind. When she wrote a history of women, she detailed the various advances made by many oppressed people, and then commented, "It must be remembered that men seize their own first, then comes woman who asks more or less tactfully, What about me?"[4]

Why *only?* What about me? Women were beginning to ask these questions all over the world, particularly in western civilizations. The Mormon women, pioneers in the valleys of Utah and other areas where they had been sent to colonize, were second to none of their day in pondering these questions and searching for reasonable answers.

They knew the history of the world, and the history of women. They were highly literate. Eliza R. Snow, their poetess and leader of their woman's organization, the Relief Society, for two decades, wrote in 1840:

> I visit Grecia's Turkish coast,
>   Long, long in darkness chain'd,
> While superstition's sombre ghost
>   O'er intellect has reign'd.

---

[3]*Ibid.*
[4]Susa Young Gates, "Women in Modern Times," p. 23, Typewritten MS, Church Archives, Historical Department, The Church of Jesus Christ of Latter-day Saints, Salt Lake City, Utah, hereinafter cited as LDS Church Archives.

Eliza R. Snow (1804-1887), first secretary and second general president of the Relief Society, poet, organizer, speaker.

> There female character, unfreed
> From bigotry's control,
> Too well attests Mohammed's creed
> That "woman has no soul."[5]

The entire history of their sex was a subject of great interest to these women. "Every step of human progress," they wrote, "from brutal savagism to the present state of civilization in Europe and America, has been accompanied by the loosening of the chains of an unholy tyranny, enabling woman to advance to a loftier position and a happier sphere."[6]

What was the "brutal savagism" of which they spoke? And how did the progress occur? An essay in the *Relief Society Magazine* gives a concise picture:

> The barriers that confronted woman through the ages were numerous and gigantic. . . . No great strides were made during the hectic days of women's hard fought revolution; but when the dust of the conflict had died down, out of the echoes of the blows struck came recognition to be given, and the first faltering steps of progress were achieved. . . .
>
> It is surprising when one casts his view back over the scenes of centuries of history, to perceive how civil law, church dogma, and tradition-breeding superstition, have held woman in leash. Those into whose hands were placed the keys of refined education, and the replenishing of the world's population after war, disease and famine, were but chattels in the eyes of the law. Woman was the outcast, the breeder, before the Church; and but the spineless, the ignorant, the evil and the inferior, in the shady mind of tradition. It is not surprising that the progress was slow; the real surprise is that it started at all.
>
> The rebellion of woman was bound to come. Flourishing Greece trembled at the first concerted women's movement lasting two centuries; and fast on its heels followed another in Rome. The former was for a political status; the latter, to gain some opportunity for education with political aims in the background. Before the young Jewish enthusiast was born in Bethlehem, woman had made two bold attempts to throw off the injustices put upon her sex and had thronged the Forum in Rome, picket-

[5]Eliza R. Snow, *Poems*, Vol. I (Liverpool: F. D. Richards, 1856), pp. 79, 80.
[6]G. A. A., "Simething About Women," *Young Woman's Journal*, 11 (March 1900), 123.

ing its entrances to petition their cause, much to the consternation
of the Consuls. Success attended their efforts; and man, ever
generous but condescending, paid them tribute by Cato the Elder,
in an immortal oration that praised the zeal but failed to sense
the significance of the cause.

Came a young man from the East with a philosophy of
equality that could forgive even an adulteress. He commended
in woman all virtues, admired her faith and charity, and up-
rooted the rank weeds of superstition. But he did not live to die
old, for the choice was not Jesus the Christ, but Barrabas. Christi-
anity overspread western Europe, but instead of unchaining women it added temporarily to their fetters; for it bore with it the
bitter view that because woman had been the instrument of
original sin, penitence and obedience to the stronger sex were her
portion in life.

Centuries passed, with women still fighting for learning.
As the Italian Renaissance flowered, the women of Italy developed
also. Too swift to endure, success came. The Latin countries
of France, Spain, and Portugal followed the example of Italy.
Women stepped into the seats of learning, teaching in universities
while men sat as students in the classes. Poets and authors, and
doctors of medicine they became; and into the labyrinths of law
they penetrated, till from their efforts in this latter sphere rings
down the ages the oration on "Mercy" by a real or fancied Portia.
Were she but a conception of man, still his instrument was a
woman, and in Italy, where woman's emergence had begun, these
tributes to woman arose.

In those times queens were renowned for their learning, were
patrons of art, swaying for decades literature and painting. Con-
vents for women and girls yielded forth educators and Mother
Superiors noted for unusual talents as well as for piety. Long
before Luther burnt the Papal bull came the first whisperings
of rebellion against the unacceptable edicts of the Church from
a Mother Superior. Let those who doubt read of St. Theresa.

Such success, however, was too rapid to endure. One by one
the universities closed their doors to women, and by the end
of the golden days of Renaissance, women stood on the steps of
universities, knocking vainly for admission. From the very university where women had taught, the University of Bologna,
the Faculty in 1377 sent forth the decree that impaled women
again on the cross of superstition, erecting barriers against her
that seemed permanent: "And whereas woman was the foundation
of sin, the weapon of the devil, the cause of man's banishment
from Paradise; and whereas, for these reasons all association

with her is to be diligently avoided; therefore do we interdict and expressly forbid that any one presume to introduce in the said college any woman whatsoever, however honorable she may be; and if anyone should perpetrate such an act, he shall be severely punished." Thus, from seats of learning, went forth the excluding edicts, which governments during the days of Catholicism rigidly enforced. Leaders of the Reformation held similar views. Under Protestantism, as well as under Catholicism, women were barred from entering universities in the quest for learning.

The New World, which was to boast of liberty and equality, was discovered by a man for man's advantage. Although the discovery was financed with the jewels of a woman, Isabella of Castille, on its soil women fought a never-ceasing battle in the quest for learning. Out of the country that framed the Magna Charta and the Bill of Rights, England, came echoes of a conflict made by the Women's Rights movement, echoes that rumbled on the shores of America during the days of the American Revolution. Colonists from the old country brought the controversy with them, and here it gained in strength and purpose.

Since the early days, when the first settlers had built schools, the debate regarding female education had waxed strong; but ground was gained steadily by its supporters, although the subjects of instruction were very limited. In 1826 Boston opened a high school for boys and girls, on equal terms, but closed it two years later amidst the barrage of disapproval that was showered upon it. Then the girls too were permitted to study during the summer months only, when the boys were on the farms. Not until the college of Oberlin in [1833] opened its doors for both sexes, black and white, did the insurmountable barriers begin to collapse, and women again began to study and instruct. Oberlin was the first college to open its doors to women since the Church had closed them during the days of the Renaissance.[7]

That, in general, was the dismal history of women up until the middle decades of the 1800s. But in 1842 an event transpired that Mormon women saw as one of the most significant of all breakthroughs in the history of womankind. A new prophet arose, and turned an important key.

But let us take a closer look at the conditions existing for women in America at that time. An editorial in the *Relief Society Magazine* gives this picture:

[7]H. C. Singer, "History of the Emancipation of Women," *Relief Society Magazine*, 16 (March 1929), 148-150.

Not only were women of that time circumscribed and down-trodden, but a great many of them accepted their condition without protest. They could not be roused from their complacent lethargy and even protested when some of their number sought to throw off their shackles. Everywhere in the United States the English Common Law was in effect. It decreed: "By marriage, the husband and wife are one person in law; that is, the legal existence of the woman is merged in that of her husband. He is her baron or lord, bound to supply her with shelter, food, clothing and medicine, and is entitled to her earnings and the use and custody of her person, which he may seize wherever he may find it." In some states "married women, insane persons, and idiots were ranked together as not fit to make a will." Politically the foreigner and drunkard were accorded the right to vote, while mothers, wives and sisters were refused it. A woman could not secure a divorce from a drunken husband. A drunkard could take his wife's clothing to pay his rum bills and the court declared it was legal because the wife belonged to her husband. If the wife secured a divorce on account of the infidelity of her husband, she had to forfeit all right to the property which they had jointly earned. The husband retained control of the estate.

In 1852, the *New York Herald,* a leading paper of that time, in an editorial asked the question, "How did woman first become subject to man, as she now is all over the world?" and answered it by saying, "By her nature, her sex, just as the Negro is, and always will be to the end of time, inferior to the white race and therefore doomed to subjection; but she is happier than she would be in any other condition, just because it is the law of her nature. . . ."

Realizing conditions at this time, one can better appreciate what Joseph Smith did for women when he organized the Relief Society March 17, 1842.[8]

Some of the leading Mormon women in Nauvoo, Illinois, had told the Prophet Joseph Smith of their desire to form a ladies' society, had drawn up a constitution and submitted it to him. He responded by inviting them to meet him in the Masonic Hall over his store on the following Thursday afternoon. "I will organize the sisters under the priesthood after a pattern of the priesthood," he said. And later he commented,

8"The Key Turned for Women," *Relief Society Magazine,* 23 (March 1936), 200, 201.

Cover of a 1936 *Relief Society Magazine* depicts
the Prophet Joseph Smith turning the key to women.

"The Church was never perfectly organized until the women
were thus organized."[9]

The first several meetings of this organization, which they
decided to call "The Female Relief Society of Nauvoo," out-
lined the direction the Society was to take. They were to
discuss and to act on those subjects "which appertain to
woman's duties, influence, responsibilities, etc., etc. — whatever has a tendency to benefit and elevate society at home
and abroad."[10]

> All the aspects of a woman's life, in a widening circle, were
> well considered and given a significance far beyond any organi-
> zational program known to women previously. The home and
> the family were given their rightful establishment in the very
> center of the circle, and from the home, the women were coun-
> seled to reach out for such virtues and such accomplishments
> as might make them "examples to the world."[11]

[9]"Story of the Organization of the Relief Society," *Relief Society Magazine*,
6 (March 1919), 129.

[10]*Woman's Exponent*, 1 (June 15, 1872), 10.

[11]*History of Relief Society 1842-1966* (Salt Lake City: The General Board
of Relief Society, 1966), p. 22.

At the sixth meeting of this organization, Joseph Smith made the statement that, seen from the perspective of years, held great significance. "I now turn the key to you in the name of God, and this Society shall rejoice, and knowledge and intelligence shall flow down from this time."[12]

Joseph Smith held the keys of a new and last dispensation of the gospel with the power to administer essential ordinances and to establish necessary organizations like the Relief Society. But the sisters saw in his "turning the key" to them something far beyond an act for the benefit of the organization itself. Susa Young Gates called it "the earthly beginning of woman's emancipation."[13] In later years others wrote:

> We see the fulfilment of his prophetic words, "knowledge and intelligence shall flow down from this time." From 1842 until the present, women have steadily reached forward, growing in intelligence and power, accomplishing more and more in furthering civilization, ministering to the afflicted, upholding righteous causes and entering every field of endeavor.[14]

Among the truths reestablished by the Prophet Joseph Smith was one that the thinking of today is just beginning to approach. In a modern magazine I read that the questions women are asking of the churches today might lead us to "discover the female side of God. . . . This will be a beautiful truth. Maybe the rediscovery of the female part of human and divine nature is the new force in the land."[15]

The female part of divine nature was taught as part of the Latter-day Saint beliefs practically from the earliest days of the restored Church. A story told by Zina Huntington Young to Susa Young Gates and to many others illustrates:

> Father Huntington lost his wife under the most trying circumstances. Her children were left desolate. One day, when her

---

[12]"The Key Turned for Women," *Relief Society Magazine,* 23 (March 1936), 201.

[13]Susa Young Gates, "The Open Door for Women," *Young Woman's Journal,* 16 (March 1905), 119.

[14]"The Key Turned for Women," p. 202.

[15]Malcolm Boyd, "Who's Afraid of Women Priests?" *Ms.,* 3 (December 1974), 51.

daughter Zina was speaking with the Prophet Joseph Smith concerning the loss of her mother and her intense grief, she asked the question:

"Will I know my mother as my mother when I get over on the Other Side?"

"Certainly you will," was the instant reply of the Prophet. "More than that, you will meet and become acquainted with your eternal Mother, the wife of your Father in Heaven."

"And have I then a Mother in Heaven?" exclaimed the astonished girl.

"You assuredly have. How could a Father claim His title unless there were also a Mother to share that parenthood?"[16]

It was this teaching from the Prophet Joseph himself that doubtless inspired Eliza R. Snow to write the poem entitled "Invocation, or the Eternal Father and Mother," sung now as a favorite hymn of the Latter-day Saints under the title "O, My Father." Eliza asked and answered a vital question:

> In the heavens are parents single?
>   No: the thought makes reason stare:
> Truth is reason: truth eternal,
>   Tells me I've a mother there.
>
> When I leave this frail existence—
>   When I lay this mortal by;
> Father, Mother, may I meet you
>   In your royal court on high?[17]

Throughout the writings of the early Mormon women are frequent allusions to this Mother, about whom little was known, but whose existence was accepted as fact. They yearned to attain to the perfection that would fit them to dwell in the presence of their Heavenly Parents.

The brethren also accepted happily this new doctrine. And it was taught by the leaders of the Church. Apostle Orson F. Whitney wrote, "Man is in the image of God, male and

---

[16]Susa Young Gates, *History of the Young Ladies' Mutual Improvement Association* (Salt Lake City: The Deseret News, 1911), p. 16.
[17]Eliza R. Snow, *Poems,* Vol. I, p. 2.

female. We have a Mother as well as a Father in heaven; and to become like them is our destiny, the destiny of all human beings who enter and steadfastly pursue the proper way."[18]

With the key turned to them by a prophet of the Lord, and with a glimpse, inspiring if not complete, of the female part of Deity, the Mormon women were better prepared than most of their contemporary sisters to deal with the questions that were being raised: Why *only?* What about me? To these questions they addressed themselves with great strength.

[18]Orson F. Whitney, "Woman's Work and 'Mormonism,'" *Young Woman's Journal*, 17 (July 1906), 295.

CHAPTER 2

The Voice of the Horn

At the Jubilee celebration of the founding of the Relief Society, fifty years after the time that Joseph Smith turned the key to women, Emmeline B. Wells, editor of the *Woman's Exponent* and later general president of the Relief Society, voiced these stirring words:

> All humanity proclaims this the woman's era. Everything important tends to emphasize the fact; the spirit of woman's future destiny rests upon the sisters, and they obey the impulses of the times in which they live! The voice of the horn! The fulfillment of prophecy! They repeat the hallelujah of woman's redemption that has been echoed down the ages.[1]

The "redemption of woman" that Emmeline and others spoke of certainly was closely associated with their feelings about the restored gospel with its doctrines, ordinances, and priesthood guidance. But it was broader even than that. They saw the Spirit of the Lord working throughout the world, upon all people, bringing new light and new thought to the subject of woman. And to them this new thinking was an absolutely essential part of the redemption of woman made "necessary" by the fall of Adam and Eve from a better state. Their thoughts

---

[1] Emmeline B. Wells, "Sentiments," *Salt Lake Stake Relief Society Record 1880-1892*, pp. 240, 241, Church Archives.

Emmeline B. Wells (1828-1921), editor of the *Woman's Exponent* for more than forty years, general president of the Relief Society, active worker for women's rights, mother of five children. *(Courtesy of Utah State Historical Society.)*

went back to the Creation, and many of them interpreted the situation this way:

> God, the Father of creation, made woman co-equal with man and gave them together the dominion of earth. The Scriptures say, "He created him in His own image, in the image of God created he him, male and female created he them. And God blessed them and said unto them, Be fruitful and multiply and replenish the earth, and subdue it; and have dominion over the fish of the sea, and the fowls of the air, and every living thing that moveth upon the earth." Mark you, God did not give him dominion, but them. God has always considered woman and commissioned her as he has man. He has sent his angel messengers to her, not to her husband, whenever he had a work she should perform. . . .
>
> Man, in his might and blindness has wrested from Eve's daughters their God-given rights in the dominion, hence this modern war which woman-kind is waging to obtain them back again. The struggle is surely divinely instituted and will ultimately succeed, for the world's problems today are sadly in need of the decisions of pure, high-minded, God-fearing men and *women*.[2]

Not only the sisters, but often the brethren voiced the same theme, encouraging women in the steps they were taking to overcome the conditions that came with the Fall. In 1884, on the occasion of the eightieth birthday of Eliza R. Snow, George Q. Cannon, first counselor to three presidents of the Church and editor of the *Juvenile Instructor,* wrote of the Mormon women:

> Their opportunities for usefulness are unequalled, and in every legitimate labor which they undertake they have the aid and the encouragement of the other sex. The incentive to become intelligent, to comprehend principle, to be strong, is greater here than in any other community that we know anything of, and I am gratified to see that our sisters are availing themselves of the grand opportunities which are furnished them for usefulness and progress. The effect of their examples upon the rising generation will be of immense value, and as the generations roll by nobler types of womanhood will be developed, until . . . she will stand side by side with man, full of that queenly dignity and self-control which will make her his suitable companion. . . .[3]

[2]Ida S. Peay, "Taking a Stand for the Right," *Woman's Exponent,* 41 (June 1913), 61.

[3]"Anniversary of Sister Eliza R. Snow Smith's Birthday," *Juvenile Instructor,* 19 (February 1, 1884), 39.

In their time, as well as in our own, the changing position of woman held dangers as well as advances. In one of the first issues of the *Woman's Exponent* Eliza R. Snow attempted a general view of the situation:

> The status of women is one of the questions of the day. Socially and politically it forces itself upon the attention of the world. Some who are so conservative that they oppose every change until they are compelled to accept it, refuse to concede that woman is entitled to the enjoyment of any rights other than those which the whims, fancies or justice, as the case may be, of men may choose to grant her. The reasons which they cannot meet with argument they decry and ridicule, an old refuge for those opposed to correct principles which they are unable to controvert. Others, again, not only recognize that woman's status should be improved, but are so radical in their extreme theories that they would set her in antagonism to man, assume for her a separate and opposing existence; and to show how entirely independent she should be would make her adopt the more reprehensible phases of character which men present, and which should be shunned or improved by them instead of being copied by women. These are two extremes, and between them is the "golden mean."[4]

The sisters were aware of what would happen if they strayed from that "golden mean." They knew that extreme views, "if widely entertained and practiced, would uproot society, bring social chaos, and introduce another cycle of 'dark ages.' "[5] Years later Susa Young Gates observed that many women had succumbed to those dangers. She wrote:

> Human conditions and relationships are chaotic today. Women in the world and here at home have attained their majority. Many of them are giddy with their new rights, so called, and have lost their poise and balance.
>
> The occasional strident voices of dominant women in the marketplaces of the world betray the fact that too many of them have interpreted liberty in terms of license.[6]

Sensing these dangers, the Mormon women in the age of emancipation sought to keep their poise, their balance, and to

[4]Eliza R. Snow, "Woman's Status," *Woman's Exponent,* 1 (July 15, 1872), 29.
[5]*Woman's Exponent,* 2 (June 1, 1873), 5.
[6]Susa Young Gates, "Union Forever," *Improvement Era,* 33 (November 1929), 50.

cultivate the golden mean. In a later chapter we will see that they felt very strongly about placing their family responsibilities first. They were, however, undeniably thrilled to be living in "the woman's era," and devoted themselves with great energy to the things that they considered to be progress. They felt they could do much good in the world by moving into an expanded sphere that included levels of activity besides the home. One sister wrote:

> It is my opinion that why the world at large is in such a plight and state of things is because woman's voice has not been heard in the Council; it has been set at naught as a vain thing. Yes, woman, you must be in silent submission, stay at home and be as Martha, troubled about many things. But be careful, and not learn the better part like Mary, lest you get too wise, and your aspirations lead you to have a voice in public affairs.[7]

Voicing the same sentiments, another sister wrote:

> To see woman from the homestead alone is to view her from a contracted standpoint, which retards her liberty. And I believe we thus hinder her progress, for there are social questions that will never be understood until woman shall stand by the side of man to discuss them. The one will always have need of the other; they will walk together, side by side, and find completeness in each other.[8]

Emmeline B. Wells was doubtless one of the most eloquent and outspoken women of her day. Many an issue of the *Exponent* stirred the sisters with editorials containing words like these:

> Women have been designated the reserve forces of humanity, and when the right time comes they will advance to the rescue. There are many lessons yet to be learned by women, and they have need of prayerful thought and careful study that they may act wisely their noble part in the great drama of life, and that all may be done in perfect harmony with the spirit and genius of the holy priesthood. . . .

[7]Mary Ann Pratt, "Give to Those Rights to Whom Rights Belong," *Woman's Exponent,* 8 (March 15, 1880), 165.

[8]Lizzie Smith, "The Equality of the Sexes," *Young Woman's Journal,* 1 (March 1890), 176.

There have been too few laborers in the past; now, if some of the reserve forces can be brought into action, the world may advance still more rapidly. Woman has by her indifference and inactivity clogged the wheels of progress; in the awakening from her dormant condition, the workers will be doubled, and a new inspiration will be given by the admission of a new element, and the burdens of life will grow lighter when all work together on a broader platform for human progress.[9]

But it was not only women of the prominence of Emmeline B. Wells, Eliza R. Snow, and Susa Young Gates that addressed themselves to the woman question. Every issue the *Exponent* and subsequent works carried essays submitted from the general readership. Many of the sisters who contributed evidenced a similar eloquence and certainly similar feelings, as the following samples will illustrate.

A woman who entitled her piece "A Contented Wife" and signed herself H.M.W. of Salt Lake City, wrote:

Many years ago some good angel whispered to me that there was a brighter day dawning for woman . . . and I see the hand of an offended God reaching out to the assistance of His patient and long-suffering daughters, who have endured enough under the rule of ungodly men. . . . We are continually taught that we must become one in all things, and many who preach this will in the next breath (figuratively speaking) ridicule and sneer at the idea of woman's aspiring to become his equal. . . . We would advise every brother who feels frightened at the thought of their stepping out of their place, and maybe into his, to go into his closet and shut the door, and ask the Lord to show him "woman's sphere." They remind me of the unbelieving world, who refuse to investigate our principles and condemn us without a hearing. We have had plenty of examples in our own eventful history to prove what women of the right type are capable of doing; and the men who are so egotistical as to believe us all to be such dependent creatures, should read the lives of some of the "Women of Mormondom," who have learned by sad experience to trust in God and not in man. "Cursed is he who maketh flesh his arm," and those who have done this have been overthrown. So let us all see that our faith is not built upon a sandy foundation.

[9]Emmeline B. Wells, "Work and Wait," *Woman's Exponent,* 8 (March 1, 1880), 148.

Every mother who understands her mission will try to train up her children in the way that they should go, that they may become bright and shining lights; but do not in your anxiety to have them excel forget what you owe to yourself; for if you aspire to nothing above housework and trying to make home comfortable and inviting to the inmates thereof, they are apt, in their upward course to honor and fame, to look upon you as the one intended by Providence to serve them. Let mothers early impress the truth upon the minds of their children, and instead of encouraging their boys in false notions, show them the inconsistency of one sex being superior to the other when both are born of the same mother. God is an impartial Being, and created woman for as noble a purpose as He did man, and I am thankful that there are a few who are honest and generous enough to acknowledge it. Such men are deserving and will always command the love and respect of every good and noble woman.[10]

Another sister, Flora S. Hill of Beaver, wrote:

We contend that woman was not born merely to do the work between four walls. The office of wife and mother is a most noble one. There are certain duties in special circumstances of life which she cannot ignore; but why confine all to the special sphere of taking care of home? A true woman —especially one who is acquainted with the design of God in the last days, and who understands so well the glory of being a mother — that woman, we expect, will never neglect her family to obtain public honor.

A great many get this question very mixed up. We feel a sincere pity for those who are so much prejudiced by traditionary ideas they cannot treat it with a clear, unprejudiced mind.

We are acquainted with certain gentlemen whom it worries very much. They fear it is going to subtract from their own dignity for women to hold office or get into very remunerative employment. Superiority is such a sweet thing. Some people take and suck it like a sugar plum. A good woman will give honor where it is due; never fear that.

Woman is not losing sight of the object of her creation when she steps forth to engage in pursuits and professions distinct and apart from home. This is a momentous age. Art and science are making wonderful strides. Everything, it would seem, which can benefit and interest the human family, is being developed and

---

[10]H. M. W., "A Contented Wife," *Woman's Exponent,* 8 (March 1, 1880), 54.

improved. Woman cannot help feeling the impulse given to this generation. It is the spirit of God, and woman shares the influence. She is bound to rise, and no human power can stop her progress.[11]

From the pen of Lucinda Lee Dalton, a pioneer schoolteacher in St. George, came this colorful essay. She is replying to a gentleman who says he "can give no good reason why women's liberties should not be as broad as man's, only — it would not suit his ideas."

But I know several good reasons in favor of women's equality in law, and they suit me passing well.

First, it would be better for women; and this fact includes

Second, it would be better for men; and both these reasons lead to

Third, it would be better for children. . . .

Woman, born to an inheritance of noble responsibilities, educated to be a citizen, knowing that an even half of the world's weal and woe lies in her hands, debarred from no pursuit for which her talents fit her, treated by her brother man as a friend and co-worker, instead of at first a goddess and next a slave — I say women so situated could not be frivolous, giddy, fickle, and the long etcetera of kindred adjectives now so often applied to her. Having a prospective field for the exercise of all her noblest powers, in the very nature of things must tend to develop just those qualities and give them strength to outgrow the inferior ones. Added respect must give her added dignity, and freedom foster her patriotism, and elevate her whole character above petty follies and narrowmindedness.

If it be objected that Republican citizenship has failed to do all this for men, I candidly admit the fact, and proceed to state what I conceive to be the reason.

I do not for one moment claim that liberty would greatly ennoble women if it were possible for her to possess it herself, and at the same time condemn her brother man to wear a ball and chain; and this, figuratively speaking, is just what the man has done. On emerging from monarchial and other despotisms he has broken his own manacles and given his own limbs nature's freedom, but still assures the woman that nature intended her to

[11]Flora S. Hill, "The Impulse of the Hour," *Woman's Exponent*, 8 (April 15, 1880), 171.

wear manacles, and made her wrists and ankles slender on purpose to fit them; that they are eminently becoming to her, and
that she would look immodest and altogether displeasing to
him without them; and he beseeches her, in the name of his
approval and the eternal fitness of things, to wear them gracefully.
But since he cannot leave her behind, his own liberty loses half
its value, and his progress toward perfection is still very slow.
At best, and in individual cases, he takes her by the hand and
assists her what he can, deeply pities her weakness and in-
capability, and considers her extremely fortunate in having him
for her guide, protector and owner.

Oftener, he lays his baggage on her back and runs lightly
on, making frequent pauses to allow her lagging steps to draw
near. During these pauses he visits the pleasure-gardens and
refreshment-stands on either hand, but decides compassionately
that since merely walking the straight thoroughfare makes her
so tired it would be the height of folly for her to think of adding
to her already severe tasks and exerting her already failing
strength in making any of these detours which do not weary him
because he is so peculiarly adapted to just that kind of activity.

One human being may aggrandize himself by oppressing
another, but he cannot thus ennoble himself. . . . Liberty, knowledge and integrity are three things which are never lessened by
being imparted to others; so let woman advance all she can in
patriotism, learning, dignity and every good word and work, and
it will detract nothing from men's abilities, acquirements, or
opportunities, but only increase the sum total of the world's
intelligence and worth.

This brings me to "Third, it will be better for children."
The children are the mother's peculiar charge, and freely does
she endow them with whatever is hers to bestow — her time,
strength, manners, mind, morals and education; if they are little,
it is but little she can give, while if she has much, much she will
bestow.

When she is a patriot, a vigilant watcher of national and
local policy, and forms intelligent opinions concerning "men and
measures," how readily her children may acquire premises from
which to draw just conclusions for themselves on the noblest and
best of sciences, human government; and how early and thoroughly
they may become imbued with the love of humanity, the best and
surest indication of a great and noble soul. I aver, from the best
procurable evidence, both positive and inferential, that children
will be born better organized and endowed both physically and
mentally when the artificial barriers between father and mother

are swept away; when the greater contentment, the deeper cultivation, the broader development, the higher elevation of mothers — and fathers — will so richly endow their offspring with great aspirations and powerful intellects that the race of today will be mere pigmies beside them.[12]

Each woman would have answered the question, "What is it you are asking for?" differently. One woman gave this comprehensive statement:

> And yet we are asked what we want that we have not already gotten, as if we were importunate children clamoring for the sweet meats that are supposed to be too strong for our digestion.
>
> We want an open field and no favor; we want you to decide upon the merits of our case and not out of a spirit of chivalry to our sex, but upon those principles of equality that grow out of the maxim, "what you would that others would do unto you, do ye even so unto them." We want equal and exact justice, we want for our girls the same chances in the race that are provided for our boys. We want to be allowed to decide what our sphere is, and not be advised by every quack in law or theology that "it is not decent for a woman to speak, and that if she thirst for knowledge she must ask her husband at home." We want capacity to be the test of power. We believe that "taxation without representation," is tyranny now, as much as it was a hundred years ago. We want to pay our taxes like honest citizens, but we want a voice in the uses to which they are to be put. We want all the schools that are supported by the Government to admit girls as well as boys. We want all churches that claim to be anything but Pagan in their doctrines to open their doors to women and men alike. We want the right of trial by juries of our peers. We want our colleges to admit young women to the same course and on the same conditions as they do young men. All these things, and many more, we ask in the name of common humanity, and we will not be contented with the half loaf that is being grudgingly offered.[13]

In verse, as well as in prose, the Mormon women responded to the "voice of the horn." The poems that appeared in their publications were themed to many subjects, but one that occurred again and again was the emerging of a new

---

[12]L. L. D. [Lucinda Lee Dalton] "Our Opinion," *Woman's Exponent,* 8 (February 15, 1880), 138.

[13]"An Address," *Woman's Exponent,* 8 (February 15, 1880), 143.

day for women. Some of these poems were reprinted by women in other parts of the nation in their own publications. The poems generally are very long, and the following are only stanzas taken from the complete pieces.

SIMPLE JUSTICE — WOMAN'S RIGHT

Is it not truly a wondrous stride
That man has stepped down from his stately pride
To discuss for woman the right and wrong
When woman has suffer'd the last so long?
Were her aims more selfish, less kind her soul,
There would be some limit to man's control;
But busied with labor that love doth bring,
She hath yielded her rights to creation's king.
Forgetful of self, amid affection's cares,
She has yielded to bondage unawares.
'Tis strange, while the world still grows and thrives,
So little is claimed by mothers and wives.[14]

— Emily Hill Woodmansee

BEHOLD THE DAWN

Man's justice is tardy and sparsely given!
But the Rights of Women are dear to Heaven!
And a brighter Era will woman see:
Behold the Dawn of her Destiny!

Is anything new, beneath the Sun?
Oh yes, in the West hath the Day begun;
The dawn of Right in the West appears
That shall brighter glow with the strength of years.

"The primitive Curse" is enough to bear,
And the women of Utah the first will share
"The honors" with men nor content they'll be
Till Women all over the earth are free.[15]

— Emily Hill Woodmansee

---

[14]Emily Hill Woodmansee, "Simple Justice — Woman's Right," *Woman's Exponent*, 8 (February 1, 1880), 129.
[15]Emily Hill Woodmansee, "Behold the Dawn," *Woman's Exponent*, 9 (October 15, 1880), 73.

Emily Hill Woodmansee (1836-1906), nationally
published pioneer poet, mother of ten children.
(Courtesy of Utah State Historical Society.)

WOMAN ARISE!

Oh woman, arise! this glow in the skies
Betokens the advent of morning;
Thy spirit should smile, exulting the while
In the day which has published its warning.

Thy desolate cry through ages gone by
To the ear of thy God has ascended;
He bids thee prepare thy armor to bear,
For soon shall thy penance be ended.

Full soon shalt thou stand co-equal with man,
Untrammeled, yet faithful and lowly,
Triumphantly meek, resistless though weak,
A conqueror, guileless and holy.

When no more a slave, be noble and brave,
But keep thy heart holy and tender.
All attributes sweet be wary to keep
Nor yield them to grandeur and splendor.[16]

— Lu Dalton

BATHSHEBA

It happened thus: In days of midnight gloom,
When vision was closed and no prophet nigh,
That the Father of woman cleft the sky,
And bade her arise from her living tomb —
Traditional servitude; and place
Her foot on the dismal ignorant past,
Stifling the cry — inferior caste;
Work her way up, flinging off the disgrace
Of innocent weakness; by study and faith,
Preparing herself, maintaining her right
To share in dominion, honor, and might;
As daughters of God, here wisdom, which saith:
"Cultivate prudence, be chaste and discreet,
Put on your strong armor, intelligence.
Lo, woman and man are omnipotence."
Awake! All her kind the morning star greet,
Henceforth by his side, no more at his feet,
Co-equal with him, his God sent helpmeet.[17]

— Ruth M. Fox

---

[16]Lu Dalton, "Woman Arise!" *Woman's Exponent,* 3 (June 15, 1874), 10.
[17]Ruth M. Fox, "Bathsheba," *Young Woman's Journal,* 20 (June 1908), 243.

Thus were Mormon women hearing and responding to the voice of the horn which heralded a new era for womankind, and responding not only with their words — but with their actions as well. Emmeline B. Wells wrote:

> That great events are about to transpire in which woman will perform an active and important revolutionary part we are not afraid to predict. The great question is, Is she preparing herself for the position she is destined to occupy and the work which will consequently devolve upon her?[18]

In subsequent chapters we will see what these women were doing to prepare themselves for this new and challenging position.

---

[18]Emmeline B. Wells, "Women's Organizations," *Woman's Exponent*, 8 (January 15, 1880), 122.

CHAPTER 3

Other Eves

The Mormon women of the age of emancipation felt strong bonds with the women across their own nation, and in fact throughout the world, who were responding to the same impulses. In 1899, as editor of the *Young Woman's Journal,* Susa Young Gates wrote of the women who had dedicated themselves to the cause of advancement for women:

> These women, oh these heroines, these Eves! For us, oh sister, for you and me, happy sheltered wives and mothers, these loving, high souls have, long before they took their bodies here on earth, consented to pluck the forbidden fruit of knowledge and experience, and to hold uncomplainingly in their mouths the apple which has too often turned to ashes upon their lips. That you and I might be able to come into our divine inheritance of perfect equality with man, they have pioneered the way, have marked the long and difficult road with precious blood from their bleeding, toilworn feet; for us they have hewn down the trees which kept our eyes from viewing God's own blue heavens; for us too have they built the bridges of public opinion across the turbid streams of prejudice and calumny. Can you and I, who are of the Second Generation, refuse to them our reverent love and constant prayerful service?[1]

Who were these great women, these Eves that Susa and other of her sisters praised so highly? Their publications

---

[1]"With the Editor," *Young Woman's Journal,* 10 (May 1899), 239.

mention with fondness many of the women of their day who were prominent on the national scene. They recognized in the person of Susan B. Anthony the "grandest Roman of them all," and followed her career with great interest. In 1873, upon receiving the news of her forthcoming trial for the crime of voting, the *Exponent* had the following scathing words for the country:

> The trial of Susan B. Anthony and fourteen other women, who cast their votes last Presidential election, and of the inspector of election who received the votes, is set for June, to be tried before the Circuit Court, at Canandaigua, New York. And the United States, which has raised the late slaves to the dignity of political sovereignty, proposes to punish, as criminals, a few of the most intelligent women in the country for exercising the right of political citizenship.[2]

Many of the Mormon women had the opportunity of meeting Miss Anthony in person at national conventions and also as the great leader traveled throughout the nation and spoke in Utah. In 1891, reporting on the Woman's Suffrage Convention, which was attended and addressed by Sarah M. Kimball, Emily S. Tanner Richards, as well as other Utah women, the *Exponent* gave this personal view of Miss Anthony:

> One finds many types of women in this great movement, and there are those who follow a certain lead, or represent a class or kind. But aside from these Miss Anthony stands out alone, a figure representative, and although a leader, in no sense of the word a copyist. Never could there be one more pronounced as distinctive from all others. It is seldom one sees such an unassuming yet queenly woman as Miss Anthony. Without having had the maternal development that adds to womanhood stars in its crown of glory, she stands pre-eminent among the women of her race and time for the valuable service she has rendered to those who were and are adding stars to the crown of motherhood. And so we say Susan B. Anthony is the mother of mothers. She has had a greater work to do than many who have borne both sons and daughters, and we pay her reverence and honor, and desire

---

[2]*Woman's Exponent,* 2 (June 1, 1873), 1.

National suffrage leaders meet with Utah suffrage leaders in 1895. Susan B. Anthony (seated center with spectacles) and the Reverend Anna Howard Shaw (standing at left with hand on chair) visited in Utah several times and maintained warm relationships with the Mormon women.

Seated, left to right: 1-Electa Wood Bullock (wife of Isaac); 2-unidentified; 3-Marie Young Dougal (wife of William B.); 4-Susan B. Anthony; 5-Phoebe Young Beatie (wife of Walter J.); 6-Zina Diantha Huntington Young (wife of Brigham); 7-Margaret A. Caine (wife of Alfred); 8-unidentified.

Standing: 1-Martha Hughes Cannon (wife of Angus M.); 2-Martha Horne Tingey (wife of Joseph S.); 3-unidentified; 4-Emily S. Tanner Richards (wife of Franklin S.); 5-Ellis Meredith; 6-Anna Howard Shaw; 7-unidentified; 8-Rebecca E. Little (wife of Feramorz); 9-Sarah M. Kimball (wife of Hiram S.); 10-unidentified; 11-Emmeline B. Wells (wife of Daniel H.); 12-unidentified; 13-Harriet Amelia Folsom Young (wife of Brigham); 14-Augusta W. Grant (wife of Heber J.); 15-unidentified; 16-Mary C. C. Bradford.

(Courtesy of Church Archives, The Church of Jesus Christ of Latter-day Saints.)

for her length of days and wide spread influence throughout America's broad land.[3]

A few years later, in 1895, Susa Young Gates wrote of the great female leader:

See what a tower of strength and force dwells in the renowned features of Susan B. Anthony; and you must not think she is a masculine woman either. She is gentle and refined in her manner, her voice is musical and even low in its tone. She has strength but not a disagreeable nor rasping way of manifesting that strength. . . .

Miss Anthony is a woman whose least favor would please and gratify even her most inveterate enemy. She is a woman much after the order of our beloved Sister Eliza R. Snow.

She is a grand woman. To know her is to be glad that God made you of the same sex as herself.[4]

In 1899 the *Young Woman's Journal* published a review of Miss Anthony's biography as written by May Wright Sewell, from which the following excerpt is taken:

Miss Anthony's entire creed rests upon her unshakable conviction of the inalienable right of the individual soul to perfect liberty, to the end that each soul may work out its own salvation according to its own conception. Few are the men and women whose names will be preserved in the annals of time who have such faith in the integrity and dependableness of the human soul. To Miss Anthony's mind, not only may the average individual be trusted, providing he first accepts a platform of human equality, to act rightly, but to her mind, trust is the very condition which will promote dependableness and integrity. . . .

Nothing will surprise the average reader of this work more than the deep religious convictions of Miss Anthony and Mrs. Stanton expressed on nearly every page of their correspondence and in the former's diaries. Both, when rejected of men, turn with unshaken confidence to the "Good Father" in whose complete knowledge of their motives and compassionate sympathy with their disappointments they apparently confide with unquestioning faith.

[3]"Representative Women of the Convention," *Woman's Exponent,* 19 (March 15, 1891), 140.
[4]Susa Young Gates, "Utah Women at the National Council of Women," *Young Woman's Journal,* 6 (June 1895), 394, 395.

The diaries of most people are traitors which expose the secret weaknesses of their authors. Miss Anthony's diary is the best possible witness of her self-forgetfulness, her magnanimity, her tenderness, her loyalty and her religious faith. Her sense of gratitude is quick, responding to every act of generosity. In a letter to a friend, acknowledging a gift, she says: "It is really wonderful how I have been carried through all these years financially. I often feel that Elijah's being fed by the ravens was no more miraculous than my being furnished with the means to do the work which has been for the past twenty years presenting itself."[5]

When Susan B. Anthony died in the spring of 1906, Mormon women felt keenly the loss of a noble soul and a true friend. Emmeline B. Wells, who in a few years would be called to serve as general president of the Relief Society, wrote this tribute to Miss Anthony:

"What shall I write? How shall I write," write of one whose memory is still fresh in the hearts of the multitudes, and concerning whom so much has been said and written in the most glowing terms? Yet in all humanity and out of my intense love for this valiant heroine of many battles, although she was a woman who loved serenity and peace, I will write what may be given me to say. . . .

Firm as the "Rock of Ages," she planted her feet upon the cornerstone of the structure commenced by the Pilgrim fathers when they fought for freedom of conscience, and in this age of the larger development of humanity, this brave, heroic woman included all the sons and daughters of the land. Neither race, nor color were excluded; there was no privileged class in her category. All were to be free; there must be no slaves in these United States. . . .

Miss Anthony began her public life as a teacher in a Quaker family for one dollar a week and board. Afterwards when she was receiving eight dollars a month, while men received from $24 to $40, she was taught her first lesson in woman's rights. During the fifteen years she devoted to teaching she made many strong pleas for the recognition of equal rights for women, in all honors and responsibilities, and for higher wages. About the same time the anti-slavery agitation began and the Anthonys and other families adjacent took an active part in the movement. Miss

[5]"The Life and Work of Susan B. Anthony," *Young Woman's Journal,* 10 (November 1899), 518.

Anthony joined in the activity both for anti-slavery and temperance. She was made secretary of the Daughters of Temperance. At a supper given by this society she made her first platform address on the question. When she was teaching in the academy she was signalized by the villagers as "the smartest woman in Canajaharie." This was in 1846. In 1852 she was sent by the Daughters of Temperance to a state mass meeting of the Sons of Temperance at Albany. During a discussion among the men she rose to speak, but was not allowed to do it. I have heard her tell the story more than once in her own humorous style. The women present were horrified and indignant and called her, "the bold thing." The President of the meeting with all the dignity he could command informed her that women were not expected to speak in meetings but only to be spectators. He meant to settle the question forever but the rebuke acted like a firebrand to one of Susan's temperament, and she marched out of the hall, half a dozen others following, to the residence of Lydia Mott, a cousin of Lucretia Mott, where they held an indignation meeting. They decided to call a woman's temperance meeting, the next evening in one of the churches, and Thomas Weed, a lifelong friend of Miss Anthony's, published notice of it in his paper.

It was during these years of active work that Miss Anthony determined to work for greater freedom for women, and decided that in order to succeed they must have the privilege of the franchise. She allied herself with the suffrage movement, leaving other reforms largely to her co-workers. About the same time she met Elizabeth Cady Stanton and formed the friendship that continued until Mrs. Stanton's death.

At a state teachers' convention held in Rochester in 1853, Miss Anthony claimed the privilege of speaking. There were many women teachers present, but none of them had a word to offer. The question under discussion was "Why is the profession of teaching not as much respected as that of lawyers, doctors and ministers?" A lively debate followed. Miss Anthony's request to be heard was at last granted. She said,

"Mr. President and Gentlemen: I have listened with attention to your discussion and I do not think you comprehend the cause of this disrespect for teachers. So long as society says woman has not the brains to be a lawyer, a preacher, or a doctor, but has sufficient brains to be a teacher, do you not see that every man of you who condescends to teach school actually acknowledges that he has no more brains than a woman? . . . "

To relate how she trudged from door to door, to secure signatures to petitions for the ballot and equal rights for women, and encountered some of the most scathing insults of her whole career would be too long a story.

Early in 1863 Miss Anthony and her colleague, Mrs. Stanton, issued a call for a meeting of the loyal women of the nation; and on May 14, an immense audience met in the Church of the Puritans in New York City. A Woman's National Loyal League was formed for the emancipation of the negroes and declared itself in favor of equal rights for women.

In 1871, Miss Anthony in company with Mrs. Stanton crossed the continent to California and visited Utah *en route*. These ladies lectured in Salt Lake City in the Old Tabernacle. It was there I first saw and heard them. There are many very interesting personal things concerning these world-famous women I should like to tell but this article is already very long. Miss Anthony has been connected with all the greatest movements that concern women. At all times she has been a conspicuous figure, and in later years has received great honors in America, and in foreign lands, and above all else has won the true love of the people wherever she was known.

On Sunday, March 11, 1906, she said to Miss Shaw, "To think I have had more than sixty-six years of hard struggle for a little liberty, and then to die without it seems cruel." Dr. Shaw replied, "Your legacy will be freedom for all womankind after you are gone. Your splendid struggle has changed life for all women everywhere." Miss Anthony responded, "If it has I have lived to some purpose." She died March 13th, 1906.[6]

At that same time the general board of the Young Ladies' Mutual Improvement Association published in their journal these "Resolutions of Respect to the Memory of Susan B. Anthony":

WHEREAS, The members of this association do feel a personal loss in the death of humanity's uncrowned queen, Miss Susan B. Anthony, and,

WHEREAS, The beauty and glory of her life have become a part of the heritage of the ages; and through that life every woman's intelligence and freedom have been augmented in an incalculable degree; and therefore, every man born of woman has had his own horizon enlarged, his possibilities increased, and his character ennobled; and,

---

[6]Emmeline B. Wells, "Susan B. Anthony, Reformer and Philanthropist," *Young Woman's Journal,* 17 (May 1906), 209-213.

WHEREAS, her Christ-like, unselfish devotion to life's highest ideals, and her accurate appreciation of justice, which never steeled her heart to the pleadings of mercy, have set a goodly pattern for us to follow; and,

WHEREAS, her passing is as fruitful and beautiful as was her living;

NOW, THEREFORE, BE IT RESOLVED, That we, the members of this association, do consecrate one hallowed niche in each individual memory wherein to place the life work of Susan B. Anthony, the supreme leader of womankind in modern historical times; and that we will endeavor to let her pure life-passion so enrich our own souls that wherever her spirit may be hidden in the bosom of eternity she shall be filled with some measure of divine joy that we do remember and that we do progress because of her life and its labors.

Our hearts are lifted, therefore, in one united hymn of praise and joy, and we offer our pleading petition to that God who doth judge the quick and dead, that in the heavenly home, to which some day we all shall go, we may be permitted to mingle and labor in the eternal verities over there, side by side with Susan B. Anthony.[7]

The passing of years did not erase Miss Anthony and her work from the minds of the Mormon women. Occasional references to her are found in their publications for decades, such as this poem printed in the *Relief Society Magazine* in 1933:

SUSAN B. ANTHONY

True Seeress of a nation's need,
Acute in thought, sublime in deed;
Her soul's invincible surmise
A starry banner in the skies
Vouchsafing truth and liberty
And franchise with equality.
By grace of God, a boundless good
To free, untrammeled womanhood!

Behind her footsteps, flowers rise
In splendor 'neath joy-smiling skies,
Where barefooted through thistle field

---

[7]Susa Young Gates and Ann M. Cannon, "Resolutions of Respect to the Memory of Susan B. Anthony," *Young Woman's Journal*, 17 (May 1906), 208.

She fared to plant their shining yield.
Stern years of travail did not tire
Her honor-angered valor fire
Whose toils bequeath to you and me
A wondrous woman legacy!

Bright dream incarnate in her blood!
Fair boon to slighted sisterhood!
Her quenchless zeal to do and dare —
Loose ancient fetters, quell despair!
Storm-mountain hooded in gray mist,
Transfigured now and sunset kissed,
Men deem her fair (though once they hissed),
Sister, Seeress, Suffragist![8]

— Minnie I. Hodapp

Another of the "bright stars shining in woman's firmament" that the Mormon sisters spoke of with fondness and admiration was Mrs. May Wright Sewell. Susa Young Gates said of her:

> Mrs. Sewell might be spoken of as the second one of that trio of peerless organizers and leaders which began with Susan B. Anthony and carried over to the present day in Mrs. Carrie Chapman Catt. Dominant, infinitely resourceful, charming in her manner, intellectual without pedantry, brilliant and witty without petty spite or sarcasm, rigorous in her devotion to duty, she was as perfect a leader as this age of women has produced.[9]

Susa had spent a week at Mrs. Sewell's home, had visited there several other times, and so was able to observe the woman closely. "Her stately courtesy and beautiful hospitality," wrote Susa, "is one of my rich memories."[10]

> Her father was a man of great independence of view; he was an abolitionist, and a believer in the equality of women, and in the highest possible education for girls. Small wonder that his brilliant daughter should add to her other gifts that of the widest humanitarianism. Small wonder indeed when a father trains his daughter to stand on a level with his own eyes that

---

[8]Minnie I. Hodapp, "Susan B. Anthony," *Relief Society Magazine,* 20 (August 1933), 481.

[9]Susa Young Gates, "Mrs. May Wright Sewell," *Relief Society Magazine,* 7 (September 1920), 499.

[10]*Ibid.,* p. 500.

hers should look into the heart of humanity with no trace of self-abasement.[11]

Lucretia Mott was another of the pioneers in the field of progress for women whose career the publications of Mormon women documented from time to time. Mrs. Mott, along with Elizabeth Cady Stanton, had attended the World Anti-Slavery Convention in 1840, and they were told, after having made the long journey, that as women they could take no official part in the proceedings but could participate as observers only. The anger and frustration this caused in them both led them to the conclusion that there was another group of human beings whose liberty needed attention besides the black slaves. From this time on they devoted themselves to the cause of women, and from their work came about the significant Seneca Falls Convention of 1848, the launching pad of the women's rights movement, and the issuance of a declaration of independence for women. This document pointed out that "the history of mankind is a history of repeated injuries and usurpations on the part of man towards woman, having in direct object the establishment of an absolute tyranny over her."[12]

The *Exponent* printed a tribute to Mrs. Mott's "superior intellectual ability, to her moral courage, to the statesman-like qualities, and to the decisive part she took in shaping and carrying forward great national movements, while at the same time she maintained the most beautiful home life."[13]

Among other of the prominent women that the sisters from Utah met at national conventions was Lucy Stone, one of the first to become identified with the crusaders in the conflict for woman's rights. The Mormon women who observed her commented:

> She is of a motherly type, and yet she stands somewhat alone, though a woman of family. She made herself a name that

[11]Susa Young Gates, "The Recent Triennial in Washington," *Young Woman's Journal,* 10 (May 1899), 213.

[12]Rose Tremain, *The Fight for Freedom for Women* (New York: Ballantine Books Inc., 1973) p. 22.

[13]"Lucretia Mott," *Woman's Exponent,* 9 (December 15, 1880), 107.

was known throughout the land in the Anti-Slavery commotion, and did not change it even in marriage, and yet her union with Mr. Blackwell is a most happy one.[14]

Of the Reverend Anna Howard Shaw the Mormon women observed:

> She possesses indomitable energy and great vigor of mind and body, and not only has the courage of her convictions, but is able to present her ideas and views as vigorously and as ingenuously as any ordained minister of "the male persuasion" could possibly do with fifty years of practice.[15]

Other nationally active women that the Utah sisters worked with and admired were Julia Ward Howe, Rachel Foster Avery, Mary F. Eastman, and many others. The Mormon women grew to love these other Eves who were devoting themselves to bettering the world in behalf of women, and were also loved by them. Bonds of sisterhood developed that extended past boundaries of geography and religion.

The challenge left by Susa Young Gates in the essay with which this chapter began will serve well to end it. Certainly the spirit of these lines is needed today. Susa envisions what one of these modern Eves would speak to her later sisters:

> She would gently speak of trials borne, but would not name the authors of her affliction. But with Christ-like meekness she would whisper, "Forgive them, my children, they were blinded by prejudice, by fear of unknown terrors and by centuries of tradition." Then with words of burning inspiration she would say, "Ye are all . . . Eves again in that ye must know in part or full the lessons I have learned so painfully. One thought I would that ye should cherish ever in remembrance of my own life: be helpful! Oh, be helpful! Hopeful and helpful! If thou see one of our own sex haughty, cold and indifferent, love her into peace and sweet unselfishness! And how much more shall ye cherish those who are struggling with the burdens I have borne . . . no matter what her color or creed. . . . The world has had its fill of hate, of envy, of blind, unreasoning prejudice; we

[14]"Representative Women of the Convention," 140.
[15]*Ibid.*

need love and sympathy far more than we do gold or precious handiwork." And in closing the sweet exhortation this Eve would add: "Pour out, then, daughter, pour out thy very soul in love to all thy sisters, and thy praise and gratitude to God that He has sent unto this Generation women who dare to pluck the fruit of knowledge, and dare to take part in teaching all mankind how to reach the perfect Inheritance."[16]

---

[16]Gates, "With the Editor," 240.

CHAPTER 4

The True Helpmeet

It was only natural that the women involved in pushing outward the borders of woman's sphere should ask the question, "What will this do to my family relationships, to my feminine attractiveness?" There were differences of opinion then, as there are now, as likely there always will be. But by and large the Mormon women felt that, wisely used, the new opportunities available to women would strengthen the family and increase the quality of the man-woman relationship. The Young Ladies' Mutual Improvement Association received this idea in a lesson designed around the concept of "home companionship":

> This change in the status and attitude of woman naturally makes a change in the type of companionship within the home: it naturally brings with it the possibilities of grave dangers to the welfare of the family group. However, if the change is recognized by both men and women as a natural change, if its possible dangers are foreseen, then it can only result in a finer type of companionship than was ever possible in the old days of woman's more restricted sphere.[1]

It is practically impossible to evaluate the success of a marriage from the outside. It would be interesting to be able to observe what really goes on by way of satisfaction in a

---

[1]"Home Companionship," *Young Woman's Journal,* 40 (September 1929), 643.

relationship under the various concepts of what a man must be and what a woman must be. Individual tastes and individual needs have always and will always vary widely. But it seems reasonable to accept the conclusion of these women on the frontier of social change that a wider sphere and a higher status for women did not damage the marriage relationship, and indeed could be a great asset. I came upon the address given by Heber J. Grant, president of the Church, at the funeral of Emily S. Tanner Richards, one of the Mormon women who had been actively involved in the women's rights movement, had addressed national conventions, and had filled her life with significant service to Church and to humanity. "Of all my near and dear friends," President Grant said, "I know of no couple, husband and wife, that during the fifty years of my acquaintance seemed to be more like one than they were. . . . I know of no more devoted husband and no more devoted wife."[2]

The age-old concept that a man could not truly love a woman who was in any way his equal was being challenged. Women were not content to be less than they might be. And men — those, at least, who were sufficiently secure — assisted them, finding that a woman who made more of herself had that much more to give to them. In an article that summarized the ideas of a number of men on "What Men Admire in Women," these comments appeared:

> The admirable woman is the "bird in the bush" who is capable of flight. Her present utility may not be that of the bird in the hand — she has a future. No woman will long be admired by man if her life can be fully circumscribed, her limitations fixed, her possibilities stated. No, she must be forever revealing new interests, new possibilities, new powers. Men admire only those objects which are capable of attracting and of holding the attention — moving, changing, and living things. The admirable woman is a progressive woman. She is admired, not only for what she is, but for what she is capable of becoming.[3]

---

[2]*In Memoriam: Emily S. Tanner Richards* (n.p. n.d.), p. 51. Quotation is from funeral address of Heber J. Grant.

[3]"What Men Admire in Women," *Young Woman's Journal,* 32 (March 1921), 139, 140.

Emily S. Tanner Richards (1850-1929), active
in Church and community, devoted to the cause
of women's rights, led Utah's delegation to the
National Suffrage Victory Celebration in 1920.
Shown here with husband Franklin S. Richards, also
a prominent leader. *(Courtesy of Utah State Historical Society.)*

A new concept of femininity, of womanhood, was being forged that was really quite revolutionary. The *Exponent* printed an extract from Grace Greenwood's address in behalf of the Lady Graduates of the Washington Business College, given in June of 1870:

> It is now pretty generally admitted that a woman may know something of business — of bookkeeping, banking, and even law — without losing the peculiar charm and beauty of her womanhood; that such studies as are pursued here do not necessarily rub the bloom from the peach of maidenly innocence, the frost from the plum of reserve, the gold-dust from the wings of the feminine soul. True womanhood is not to be essentially changed by changed pursuits and conditions. There is a tough vitality about tender womanhood. It is a tree, whose roots take hold on eternal life.[4]

Henry Ward Beecher was one of the gentlemen of the day that was writing a good deal about the expanding sphere of women. The sisters quoted him in the *Exponent,* saying, "The following ideas are sound and correct, and it is a pity that all men do not think with Beecher on the subject in question."

> People fear the effect upon the family if women should vote and think. They think that the tenderness and sweetness of the family relation has something to do with weakness. It has much to do with fineness, but not with weakness. It is not the fact of woman's looking up to a man that pleases him — it is that in her that looks up. . . . A greater freedom for woman will not unsex her. . . . Does it take away taste and destroy refinement to ponder deeply? Make mothers more and you make their children more. You will not make them coarse by giving them power. Is God coarse because he is infinite? That which the family needs more than anything else is a higher state of womanly development.[5]

The question of maintaining individuality in marriage is inherent in the whole subject of woman's sphere. The Mormon women of the decades of emancipation felt that

---

[4]*Woman's Exponent,* 1 (July 1, 1872), 22.
[5]"Beecher on Woman Suffrage," *Woman's Exponent,* 1 (October 15, 1872), 79.

to be an individual was to be a better wife. A lesson in Relief Society put it this way:

> In this matter of making adjustments during the early years of married life care should be taken not to sacrifice individuality. True adjustment is mutual adjustment. It frequently happens that one or the other member of the union dominates in every respect to the extent that the weaker or less aggressive personality becomes a mere creation of circumstances. The fact that the man is head of the family does not imply that a woman may not have the right to live her own life.

> Again Frank Crane writes: "There are three ways of looking at a woman. You can look up and call her (with more or less mental reservation) an angel, divine and ethereal. . . . It is usually temporary and easily slumps into contempt, jealousy, and all kinds of morbidities, for it is in itself untrue and morbid.

> "Secondly, you can look downward on her. You can play the autocrat. You can emphasize your lordship and mastery. And no one but a petty soul could possibly enjoy doing this.

> "Thirdly, you can look her level in the eye, as your equal, your pal, your friend and companion."

> Proper adjustment is thus a union which respects the personality, the rights, the qualifications of each other. It is team work where each lessens the burden of the other by keeping up his own end, pulling his part of the load. It is a cooperation in which each contributes his best effort, his peculiar power unrestricted by the dominating influence of the other.

> In short, proper adjustment is one of love, a union in spirit, in purpose, one which grows in mutual understanding as to rights, privileges, powers and obligations. It leaves a man as a man, and a woman as a woman, to live as individuals, a full and complete life.

> "The happiest marriages," says Jordan, "are those where there is perfect unity and identity of view in the great essentials; perfect freedom in non-essentials, and perfect harmony even in difference of view."[6]

Mattie Horne Tingey, speaking at a women's congress in Chicago in 1893, made these remarks:

[6]"Marriage and Its Adjustments," *Relief Society Magazine,* 10 (July 1923), 369, 370.

When women entertain the idea a wife and mother advanced to me, that when she married she gave up her own individuality, she felt she had no mind nor will independent of her husband's, can we wonder that their children grow up with the idea that father and mother are one, and that one is the father? It has always roused an indignant feeling within me to hear a woman say in answer to her child's question, "O, I don't know anything about such things; go and ask your father." Every time she makes a remark of that nature the mother loses influence and the father gains it.

Let woman prepare herself to stand side by side, shoulder to shoulder with her husband in all the affairs of life, to be a wise counselor and helpmeet unto him, as her Creator designed she should be; let mothers impress upon their children the principles of justice and equal rights, and the women of the next generation will not have to beg and plead for what rightfully belongs to them.[7]

Emmeline B. Wells added these thoughts to the idea that a woman who has progressed as an individual would make a better helpmeet for her husband:

Women who have opinions of their own are able to counsel with their husbands in regard to the home and the children. They carry their own burdens along more easily than the innocent, unsophisticated, frivolous, who depend solely upon someone else's judgment all their life long. They tell us women will have to dispense with the gallantry of the opposite sex when they enter the lists with men. Then man will have to dispense with the attentions and caresses of woman which make life so pleasant. If men cannot afford to be gallant to women who are their equals in intellect and education, then women will be careful not to throw away their sweet attractions, and there will, perhaps, be more fair play than there is nowadays, and it will not be such a one-sided affair as it has been.[8]

Because woman is designed to be the eternal companion of man, the Mormon women felt that two people in a marriage relationship should not be unevenly yoked. They yearned for a true social, spiritual, and intellectual companionship.

[7]"Address of Mrs. Mattie Horne Tingey," *Young Woman's Journal,* 4 (September 1893), 549.

[8]"Agitation is Educational," *Woman's Exponent,* 8 (February 1, 1880), 132.

True intellectual companionship is possible only when husband and wife have the same standards of intelligence. Their intellectual achievements may differ as their natures and talents differ — as their work in life naturally differs. But the same standard of excellence actuates them both. A low grade of intelligence could not be happy to be always in the company of the highest; it cannot be at its best, and is oppressed by the magnitude of the other; and how wretched is the highest intelligence bound to a low grade of mind. They cannot travel together, neither be happy. The Latter-day Saint wife should interest herself in those things that interest her husband and plan for study and discussion and enjoyment of things of mutual uplift. She should seek the highest mental development in order to be worthy the companionship of a noble mind.[9]

The pioneering conditions that the early Mormon women lived under were hardly conducive to a fragile femininity. But this they looked upon as a blessing, feeling that just such conditions helped to produce "women of power and usefulness." In an essay entitled "What Pioneering Does for Womanhood," one sister wrote:

To be a woman does not mean to be a creature dressed and decorated to charm, to dazzle, to amuse; it does not mean to be a butterfly to flit on gauzy wings, but it means to be one in the creations of our Father in Heaven; it means a being created in the image of our Mother in Heaven sent to earth to gain experience that will make her more like that Heavenly Mother, to gain possession of the attributes which make her great. In a broad way the term womanhood includes such virtues. It means to have power to do all the work that lies within the sphere of woman's life. . . . There are walks in life that tend to develop that power — walks that make us strong in the power to do.

On the frontier and in rural districts the conditions are such that each must bear a certain responsibility. Many real, earnest problems — in fact, the problem of life and death confronts us. Each person of necessity feels the situation and as a result takes hold of the conditions, determined to shape them for the best good of all.

These conditions are not always the same, they vary from day to day, from hour to hour; therefore, the judgments must vary, and as the conditions are frequently not previously known one

---

[9]"Guide Department," *Young Woman's Journal,* 25 (August 1914) 520.

is compelled to judge in haste many times. Activity being called for at once, decisions must be rendered almost instantaneously, and thus the power to judge, to decide with precision, with alacrity, is developed. In many instances, too, one must be her own counselor. These are the positions the young girl must occupy, providing the mother is wise enough to place the necessary responsibility on that girl; and pardon this slight digression while I say, "Mothers, do not, by seeming kindness, rob your girls of this blessed responsibility — this responsibility intended by Heaven for her."[10]

Among the taboos for feminine deportment that were in question was that of strenuous physical activity. One sister, a frequent contributor to the *Exponent,* wrote in 1873:

Custom has long demanded for boys vigorous and healthy exercise, which is the legitimate means of giving harmonious vigor to the body. But custom has also forbidden for girls such exercise, because forsooth it is ungenteel to wrestle, run and row. . . .

It is not enough that one sex be trained to bodily strength and symmetry; that is doing the work by halves. Let the girls also have due attention on this point. And do not let all their exercises be drudgery either. Washing, sweeping and churning are all very well in their place; but if "all work and no play make Jack a dull boy," I contend that it will also make Jill a dull girl. She should learn to skate, to swim, to play ball, and — yes, to shoot! Self protection demands this last in these wild, western countries, and to my mind it would be far more pleasing to see our girl going out on shooting excursions with her brothers and sturdily bearing home at night the game she has captured, than laced up in corsets, with smelling bottle at nose, giving little plaintive screams if she should spy a mouse, or a frog, or any of God's harmless creatures which should awaken admiration for His boundless wisdom instead of fear or even disgust. It is high time that such nervous timidity, not to say such affectation, should pass into disfavor. And the very best way to accomplish this desirable end, would be to give the girl such confidence in her physical prowess that she would feel herself equal to any small contingencies.[11]

---

[10]Hannah Grover, "What Pioneering Does For Womanhood," *Young Woman's Journal,* 13 (July 1902), 315, 316.

[11]L. L. D. [Lucinda Lee Dalton], "Exercise for Girls," *Woman's Exponent,* 1 (January 1, 1873), 131.

The publications of the early Mormon women served many purposes, one of them being a forum to air differing points of view. In the *Young Woman's Journal* of 1890 I discovered an essay by a gentleman and a response by a woman that make highly interesting reading. The man, writing under a pseudonym (very common then) of "Santiago," and elsewhere identified as James H. Martineau, entitled his essay "Woman's Power." He was disturbed at the growing independence of woman and was moved to remind her that it might cost her man's love. A few statements from his article will serve to give the crux of the argument:

> Men love women because they are *women*. There it is in a nut shell — because they are women and not men, because they are not masculine in their ways, because of their womanhood. And nothing will so easily change in a man this love, so tender and true, into mere admiration and esteem, as for a woman to exchange her sweet womanly ways for the masculinity of the other sex. His love changes at once to friendship. . . .
>
> Young ladies, remember it never was intended that men and women should be alike. Woman is the complement of man — his necessary balance. Is he strong, forceful, stern, merciless, imperious, striding over all opposition? She is gentle, kind, loving, forgiving, full of mercy and charity. But each sex is endowed with those attributes it most needs. . . .
>
> So, girls, don't be mannish; cultivate your womanhood, and bind to you the hearts of those you love with bands, silken perhaps, but stronger far than steel.[12]

In the very next issue appears a response from a lady who calls herself "Skurlock":

> I fear our brisk, breezy *Journal,* born among the mountains in the great, roomy, progressive West, has come near falling into the chuckholes of the old, beaten, dusty track of those publications which from time immemorial have taken it upon themselves to give advice to the girls. . . .
>
> In times past, women have, because they loved, done many improper things; and one of them is they often preferred men's

---

[12]Santiago [James H. Martineau], "Woman's Power," *Young Woman's Journal,* 1 (August 1890), 406, 407.

opinions to their own and even yielded points of conscience for the sake of pleasing them, until very naturally they are looked upon by men as shallow, weak, and contemptible. If a certain course brings us to a certain destination, and an opposite course leads to an opposite destination, it must be that since so much consideration for men's notions have brought us into disrepute, that a course of self-reliance and self-assertion will restore our credit.

I agree with *Santiago* that men love women because they are women, and because men cannot help loving them, but I disagree with . . . him in the collateral reasons.

Is it true that men love best the weak, helpless, dependent kind of woman? I doubt it. I admit that they often think so during their own boyish days, because it so flatters the strength, power and dignity which they aspire to possess. . . .

[But] if this same youth chooses for a wife a sweet, clinging, just-as-you-say, dear, kind of a girl, it may be all satisfactory during courtship. She will stay out with him a little later than is quite compatible with health and good example; she will sit with him in the parlor a little longer than is approved by her parents and consistent with early rising and industry; she will have no conflicting opinions, no troublesome exactions in behalf of industry, temperance, morality or ambition, but will be ready to adopt any opinion he advances, and will testify her love for him by being jealous if he is not sufficiently exclusive in his attentions; she will be so weak she cannot bear the least shadow of coolness from her sun of love, so clinging she can scarcely cross the room without his arm to support her, and so timid she will faint if a mouse should run across the floor, or a cow boo at a furlong's distance — and her strong, brave cavalier will find it very delightful.

But how the table turns after marriage! Adolphus expects this same gentle creature to be ready by day or by night to minister to his comfort and pleasure, to manage the complicated household machinery without a jar, to bear, nurture and perfect children after his ideas of perfection, to always know what he will think ought to be done and do it without troubling him in the least; and if she fall short of all these perfections — well, he is a very unfortunate man.

But let us suppose he grows in wisdom as well as in years; then he sees his home and children mismanaged without the power to hinder; he has no patience with the little airs and graces which were once so charming; and deep in proportion to his self-contempt for having been a fly to be caught in a gossamer web, will be his contempt for the small fears, pretended or real, which so constantly claim his presence and guardianship. If life presents real crosses, real reverses, real need of a worker, a help-meet, the larger his own soul and the greater his need, just so much greater will be the void which her littleness cannot fill, and he knows it.

If he be large enough, noble enough, to realize that she is not to blame for the mistake he made in selecting an unsuitable wife, he will continue to treat her gently, but his love will change into pity if not contempt, lacking the "mere admiration and esteem."

"Mere admiration and esteem." *Mere* must mean *only, that and no more,* as if admiration and esteem were something inferior to and below love, but in truth so superior to and above the gross passion which usually bears the name of love that we would better say "ripen and develop into admiration and esteem. . . ."

And oh, Santiago, what is love? Esteem is a strong root, admiration is a sturdy stalk; and when this wholesome plant blossoms into tenderness, behold, we call it love. The tenderness without the admiration and esteem is at best only a cut flower which in a brief time will fade and die, leaving for its possessor only dust and ashes. . . .

"Young ladies, remember, it was never intended that men and women should be alike." Oh, most lucid Santiago, how do you construe the word *alike?* Men and women should be alike true, chaste, holy, just and faithful, if not alike weak, cowardly, treacherous and false; alike forbearing, hopeful, prudent, diligent in doing good, and full of grace and truth, if not alike in face, form, occupations and gifts.

God is the father of both, and giveth talents to be improved, not hidden in a napkin; and it is safe to say to all — follow the bend of your individual tastes and inclinations so far as circumstances will permit, and as long as they do not carry you outside of the Ten Commandments.

In conclusion permit me to say at the risk of being reminded that my first sentence complains of too much advice: Young ladies, do not do this or that, no matter how good, because it would please men, for the scripture says, "Woe to him (or her) who putteth trust in man"; but do all good deeds because they will please your Heavenly Father, the only friend who never fails the souls who trust in Him. Do not forbear to do this or that, no matter how wrong, because it will displease men, but because it will displease your Heavenly Father, and bring you low in your own esteem.

Whatever we know to be right we should do though the world oppose; not for boast, not for defiance, not for notoriety, but for the courage of our convictions, the discharge of our duty, the approval of conscience, and the glory of God. Be not mannish or womanish; be pure, be just, be saintlike; and all will be well with you in this life and in that which is to come.[13]

Throughout the writing of these Mormon women of long ago appears the belief that if they, in righteousness, made of themselves every good thing they had the capacity for, they would *have* more and *be* more, and consequently could *give* more to their families, to their husbands and their children. They envisioned that as a true helpmeet, standing at the side of, not behind her husband, a woman could better serve and better love. As expressed in a poem by one of the sisters:

> Oh, when in freedom woman's love takes flower,
> Then man shall come to birth in mighty power!
> Full-facultied at last, nor longer held
> Heredity's sad slave, by love impelled,
> Man shall behold the woman, and shall see
> His equal ever, as her equal he! . . .
>
> And power shall be given each to prove
> And know in full the endless strength of love.
> Oh! worlds and ages cannot be too vast
> For this divine experience to last![14]

[13]Skurlock, "Woman's Power," *Young Woman's Journal,* 1 (September 1890), 442-445.

[14]Valeria DeMude Kelsey, "Vision or Dream?" *Young Woman's Journal,* 25 (October 1914), 609.

CHAPTER 5

To Your Task, O Mothers!

When Louisa Lulu Greene accepted the call from Brigham Young to serve as first editor of the *Woman's Exponent* and to regard the position as a mission,[1] she was twenty-three years of age. Louisa served in this position for five years, during which time she added Richards to her name and became an expectant mother. The following note from her is found in an August 1877 *Exponent*:

> In consideration of the curiosity, and perhaps anxiety, of my friends, personal and otherwise, I give a brief explanation of my reasons for withdrawing from public service for the present. My general health is good, but my head and eyes need recruiting, and I have decided to humor them. I have also decided that during the years of my life which may be properly devoted to the rearing of a family, I will give my special attention to that most important branch of "Home Industry." Not that my interest in the public weal is diminishing, or that I think the best season of a woman's life should be completely absorbed in her domestic duties. But every reflecting mother and every true philanthropist can see the happy medium between being selfishly home bound and foolishly public spirited.[2]

---

[1]"The Pioneer Woman Editor of the Church," *Relief Society Magazine*, 12 (July 1925), 343.

[2]Louisa Lulu Greene Richards, "Valedictory," *Woman's Exponent*, 6 (August 1, 1877), 36.

This resignation of the editor would have come as no surprise to the readers of the *Exponent*. For it was an unquestioned principle among them all that while there are many excellent ways in which a woman can serve, her "greatest service to the city, state and nation is to train her children to be strong and pure men and women."[3]

This firm belief was conveyed by Brigham Young in the advice he gave to his daughter Susa. She always remembered it, and told others:

> President Young once said to me, If you were to become the greatest writer . . . the most gifted and learned woman of your time, and had neglected your home and children in order to become so . . . you will find your whole life had been a failure. . . . If, in addition to your wifely and motherly duties, you can pursue one or more fields of public labor . . . all the good that you can accomplish . . . will be so much added glory to your eternal crown.[4]

As the contributors to the publications of the early Mormon women investigated, defended, and attacked the various theories of what woman was designed to be and to do, the supreme value of motherhood was never undersold. A little piece by one who called herself "Sister Plunkett" is representative of many:

> Where is the true Sphere of Woman is a question that is agitating the public mind not a little. Well, if after careful, prayerful, honest considerations any woman thinks she can do the most good to humanity generally by entering the lecture field, the pulpit or any of the avenues of life usually filled by men — if, I say, she is convinced that here lies her life's work — then I say to her Godspeed. But be very careful, my sister, and search well your own heart, lest it be a love of notoriety, publicity and even money that leads you forth in this direction.
>
> No, no, I would not have women dead heads. I would have them educated, intelligent, pure and true. But I would have them fill the places designed for them by their Creator, for there I think they can do the most good, and exert the greatest influence.

---

[3]"Woman's Influence," *Young Woman's Journal*, 28 (April 1917), 230.
[4]"Editor's Department," *Young Woman's Journal*, 5 (June 1894), 449.

Susa Young Gates (1856-1933), editor and founder
of the *Young Woman's Journal,* later editor of the
Relief Society Magazine, member of Relief Society
general board, genealogist, active in politics, woman
suffragist. Shown here with two of her thirteen
children, Emma Lucy (left), Leah (right), and a
granddaughter. *(Courtesy of Utah State Historical
Society.)*

I would have them in HOMES, as wives and mothers, and let no one think it not a high and holy office to be a mother, to train the little ones in paths of truth and right, lead them on to virtue, guide the footsteps so they falter not, but press on to the mark of their high calling. Oh, is it not an important thing to train an immortal mind, teach it to think and act and then send it forth to do good for all coming time? 'Tis a holy work, 'tis God's work, 'tis woman's work, and for this will be given a crown of glorious immortality. . . . When she draws near to the end, when earth and earthly scenes are about to fade away, then, she will feel that she has performed faithfully the work of her Maker, that she has endeavored to be true to the position God placed her in when He created her woman.[5]

Quoting Mrs. Beecher, the *Young Woman's Journal* instructed its readers:

Let home stand first before all other things. No matter how high your ambitions may transcend its duties, no matter how far your talents or your influence may reach beyond its doors, before everything else, build up a true home. Be not its slave, but its minister: let it not be enough that it is swept and garnished, that its silver is brilliant, that its food is delicious, but feed the love in it, feed thought and aspiration, feed all charity and gentleness in it. Then from its walls shall come forth the true woman and the true man — who shall together rule and bless the land. Is this an over-wrought picture? We think not. What honor can be greater than to rule a home? What dignity higher than to reign its undisputed mistress? What pleasure greater can be insured than to preside over a true home, where husband and children rise to call you blessed? To be the guiding star, the ruling spirit, in such a position is higher than to rule an empire.[6]

Believing sincerely, as Horace Mann put it, that "one right former is worth a thousand reformers,"[7] the Mormon women reminded one another of the value of the product they were forming:

Then, mothers, pause and consider, for one moment, the magnitude of the power and responsibility resting upon you.

---

[5]Sister Plunkett, "Woman's Sphere," *Woman's Exponent,* 8 (February 1, 1880), 1.

[6]Ethelwynne Stringham Collett, "A Girl's Aim," *Young Woman's Journal,* 18 (February 1907), 73, 74.

[7]*Ibid.,* p. 74.

Remember, each one, you are arbitress of the destiny of an immortal being; and try by every means in your power to plant germs of integrity and purity instead of death and destruction.[8]

The influences we feel at home are lasting ones, as hundreds of intelligent men and women grown old in knowledge will testify. Home is the just conductor giving just ideas to the infant mind. If all is smooth, easy and pleasant at home we take the feeling out into the world with us. If all is discord, and peace has fled from the home, how terrible for the inmates. Home is our first school: there we take our first lessons in life, there our hearts glow with childish love and pity, with sympathy and affection for those who sit by our side, who share our joys and sorrows, who feel with us the trials and cares of the present life.[9]

In 1905 President Roosevelt addressed the Congress of Mothers, and the women of Utah were sufficiently impressed with his remarks that they printed them in the *Exponent*. The following is an excerpt:

The most honorable and desirable task which can beset any woman is to be a good and wise mother in a home marked by self-respect and mutual forbearance, by willingness to perform duty, and by refusal to sink into self-indulgence or avoid that which entails effort and self-sacrifice. Of course, there are exceptional men and exceptional women who can do, and ought to do, much more than this, who can lead and ought to lead great careers of outside usefulness in addition to — not as substitutes for — their home work; but I am not speaking of exceptions; I am speaking of the primary duties, I am speaking of the average citizens, the average men and women who make up the nation.

Inasmuch as I am speaking to an assemblage of mothers, I shall have nothing whatever to say in praise of an easy life. Yours is the work which is never ended. No mother has an easy time, and most mothers have very hard times. And yet what true mother would barter her experience of joy and sorrow in exchange for a life of cold selfishness which insists upon perpetual amusement and the avoidance of care, and which often finds its fit dwelling place in some flat designed to furnish with the least possible expenditure of effort the maximum of comfort

---

[8]"And Murders Increase in the Land," *Woman's Exponent*, 1 (May 1, 1873), 184.

[9]Camelia, "Home Influence," *Woman's Exponent*, 8 (May 1, 1880), 177.

and of luxury, but in which there is literally no place for children.[10]

The sisters realized that because the status given by society to man had always been higher than that given to woman, it would be tempting for many to assume that woman's peculiar attribute of childbearing could profitably be traded in for the things that men had always done. Against this they warned one another. In the words of Leah D. Widtsoe:

> Indeed a woman who would sacrifice the greatest of all earth professions, that of Motherhood which is hers by right of sex, for the senseless reason of proving that she could do a man's work as well as any man, or for any other reason, is something less than a true woman and is to be pitied as well as condemned. While on the other hand it is but a small and puny-souled man who could wish to humiliate woman as a class and keep her as the inferior sex. For men can never rise superior to the women who bear and nurture them. The man who fears the dominance of woman or suspects that she is now attempting to take revenge on man for the centuries that her sex has been held in thralldom before the law — such a man admits his own inferiority, and condemns his own beginnings.[11]

In constantly underlining the importance of motherhood, these Mormon women were not speaking only of childbearing, of maternity. They knew that providing bodies for their children was only the beginning of their responsibilities. From then on they served as model, teacher, inspirer.

> Although it is of great importance to provide food and shelter for her little one, and clothe him as well, these are the least of woman's obligations to the child she bears. Though she does these things ever so well, yet fails to inspire him intellectually and spiritually to the utmost heights of attainment, she has not earned the holy name of mother. Creatures of forest and field provide for all the physical needs of their offspring. The human spirit — image of the Creator — needs a higher care and tuition.
>
> A child's play offers the best and earliest opportunity for a mother's inspirational guidance. Any woman who is really interested in her children can find time to tell them beautiful stories,

[10]"Extracts," *Woman's Exponent,* 33 (April 1905), 79.
[11]Leah D. Widtsoe, "Priesthood and Womanhood," *Relief Society Magazine,* 20 (November 1933), 668.

to teach them interesting games, to provide for them so many simple, constructive playthings that they will have more fun at home than anywhere else. A woman really worthy of the name of mother, does not allow her children to spend all their time at the neighbors, or to run the streets from morning till night in unsupervised play, with the assertion, "My children don't worry me any. I know they'll come home when they get hungry."

How much truth do you suppose there is in this assertion made by an educator: "The child gets his intellectual inspiration and guidance from the old maid school teacher, not from the mother"? Might he not truthfully have said also, "The child's spiritual awakening comes through the church, not through the average mother and home"?

What a wonderful world we should soon have if every mother could but have the vision, the love, the determination to point and lead the way for her child to climb the supreme heights of achievement possible to him, to climb always with this ideal before him: "Each gift and talent which I possess shall be developed and shall be used in the service of humanity. I will work unceasingly for God and the glory — never count the gain." Only when nurtured by such mothers shall all little ones come into their true heritage as children of God.[12]

It was because these women realized the enormous challenge that motherhood was that they wished to make themselves equal to it by expanding the sphere of woman. Had they not printed in the *Exponent* that very potent phrase: "Make mothers more and you make their children more"?[13] From this feeling came much of their determination to destroy those unhelpful laws, traditions and social customs that had for centuries made woman less.

What then should be the training of girls, who are to bear these heavy responsibilities, and to be the mothers of the races of mankind? Can too much be done to enlighten their minds, to educate their heads and their hearts? Girls should be taught from their earliest years to qualify themselves to become worthy of the exalted office of motherhood and to choose wisely the companion who is to be the co-mate in this great work of imparting new life to an immortal being. The power to regulate civil and social conditions has not yet been equally balanced be-

[12]Jean Brown Fonnesbeck, "Motherhood vs. Maternity," *Young Woman's Journal,* 39 (May 1923), 244, 235.
[13]"Beecher on Woman Suffrage," 79.

tween men and women, but has commenced to work in a small degree, and new light is constantly dawning upon the minds of the people. Should not woman, the mother, have a voice in what should be the conditions of the society in which her sons and daughters are to be ushered? . . .

That woman's centre is the home-life, that an inviolate home is her sanctuary, we firmly and truly believe; but that she should have power to exert an instrumentality in all the departments whereby her offspring are to be protected, educated and provided for seems only rational and proper.[14]

In their great reverence for the state of motherhood, the early Mormon sisters did not ignore the importance of fatherhood. Evidently there was back then, as there is now, a feeling among many men that involvement with children, even their own, was not part of their responsibility, that breadwinning for the family was their only obligation. In 1890 the *Young Woman's Journal* carried this little anecdote:

Young Wife: "John, I wish you would rock the baby."

Young Husband: "What'll I rock the baby for?"

"Because he's not very well. And what's more, half of him belongs to you, and you should not object to rock him."

"Well, don't half belong to you?"

"Yes."

"Well, you can rock your half and let my half holler."[15]

And at another time, in a more serious vein, they wrote:

At no time has the Lord placed the obligation of training children solely on the mothers. We read in 1st Samuel that, because Eli's sons were "vile and he restrained them not," that sudden destruction was visited upon him and his house. And in the Doctrine and Covenants, Section 93, verses 38 to 44, we find that several of the brethren were rebuked for not teaching their children light and truth according to the commandments. The Lord has also said that *parents* shall be held responsible for the training of their children. (Doc. and Cov., Sec. 68; verse 25.)[16]

---

[14]"Woman and Her Duties," *Woman's Exponent,* 8 (February 15, 1880), 140.

[15]*Young Woman's Journal,* 2 (October 1890), 27.

[16]Ruth May Fox, "To Your Task, O Women!" *Young Woman's Journal,* 34 (May 1923), 284.

To be a "mother in Israel" was unquestionably the greatest honor to which these women could aspire. But there was a great deal more implied in that phrase than meets the eye. An interesting insight is given in the remarks made by Lucy Mack Smith, the mother of the Prophet Joseph, at the general conference of the Church in Nauvoo, Illinois, in 1845. As recorded in Brigham Young's Office Journal:

> She commenced by saying that she was truly glad that the Lord had let her see so large a congregation. She had a great deal of advice to give, but Brother Brigham Young had done the errand, he had fixed it completely. There were comparatively few in the assembly who were acquainted with her family. She was the mother of eleven children, seven of whom were boys. She raised them in the fear and love of God, and never was there a more obedient family. She warned parents that they were accountable for their children's conduct, advised them to give them books and work to keep them from idleness, warned all to be full of love, goodness and kindness, and never to do in secret what they would not do in the presence of millions. She wished to know of the congregation whether they considered her a mother in Israel (upon which President B. Young said, all who consider Mother Smith as a mother in Israel, signify it by saying yes! One universal "yes" rang throughout).[17]

This is interesting. Lucy, who had borne eleven children, wished to know if she was considered a mother in Israel. Another insight comes from remarks made at the funeral of Eliza R. Snow in the Salt Lake Tabernacle in 1887. Among other praise given her was the tribute voiced by many of the speakers that she was indeed a mother in Israel. When Elder John W. Taylor took his turn to speak, he said:

> We have heard the word "Mother" mentioned here. It is known among us that George Washington is called the "Father of his country" though he died without children. Yet through the devotion of the American people he has earned the name of Father. Inasmuch as the deceased was deprived of bearing children, she is entitled to be called Mother among this people, just as much as George Washington is to be called Father of the people of the United States. She has been a mother to this people.

[17]"Mothers in Israel," *Relief Society Magazine*, 3 (January 1916), 5.

... I pray God the Eternal Father that whenever we think of Eliza R. Snow Smith, we will not think of her as "Aunt Eliza" in the future, but that we may in truth and righteousness call her Mother.[18]

Eliza, who never bore a child, was considered a mother in Israel. Evidently there was more to the concept of motherhood than the biological.

In those days, as in all days, there were many good women who for various reasons did not marry and did not bear children. What of them?

The answer is simple: Motherhood can be exercised as universally and vicariously as can Priesthood. The world needs good mothers more than any other one thing. Because a woman has been denied children of her very own is no reason why her God-given power and gift may not be exercised for the countless neglected children in every community whose mothers are unfit or have been taken from earth. All intelligent worth-while work for social betterment in private life or in organized activity is but an enlarged Motherhood acting for the uplift of mankind. And in this field every would-be Mother could and should be active.[19]

The woman who has no children of her own, but whose heart is full of an all-enfolding love for children, and who loses no opportunity to inspire, to guide, to urge children onward, upward, Godward — is not such a woman more truly a mother than she who gives birth to a dozen boys and girls, yet does nothing for them but provide for their physical needs? All about us, working in every one of our church organizations, there are many lovely mothers who have no children of their own. We should see to it that they wear the white carnation on Mother's Day.[20]

This expanded concept of motherhood appears to be in harmony with the teachings of the Savior. He sought on many occasions to give a new perspective to family relationships. When the woman said to him, "Blessed is the womb that bare thee, and the paps which thou hast sucked," he replied, "Yea rather, blessed are they that hear the word of

[18]*The Life and Labors of Eliza R. Snow Smith; With a Full Account of Her Funeral Services* (Salt Lake City: Juvenile Instructor Office, 1888), p. 24.

[19]Leah D. Widtsoe, "Priesthood and Womanhood," *Relief Society Magazine,* 20 (October 1933), 597.

[20]Fonnesbeck, p. 244.

God, and keep it."[21] The same feeling exists in an incident related by Matthew:

> Then one said unto him, Behold, thy mother and thy brethren stand without, desiring to speak with thee.
>
> But he answered and said unto him that told him, Who is my mother? and who are my brethren?
>
> And he stretched forth his hand toward his disciples, and said, Behold my mother and my brethren!
>
> For whosoever shall do the will of my Father which is in heaven, the same is my brother, and sister, and mother.[22]

Whether, then, they were involved in literal maternity, or in the more extended motherhood that included "intelligent, worth-while work for social betterment in private life or in organized activity," the Mormon women of the turbulent years of female emancipation had a cornerstone for their lives that they were unwilling to trade. In the words of one of their later writers, Ruth May Fox:

> To your task, O, Latter-day Saint Mothers! May you appreciate your high and holy calling and should you at any time be tempted to shirk this great obligation, in the language of one of old, may you exclaim, "I am engaged in a great work, I cannot come down."[23]

---

[21]Luke 11:27, 28.
[22]Matthew 13:47-50.
[23]Fox, "To Your Task, O Women!" p. 286.

CHAPTER 6

Cobwebs on the Brain

"A wife will be a better wife, a mother more a mother," wrote the Mormon women, "if intellectually her husband's equal." And, "We affirm that she who cultivates virtue and dares to exercise all her mental powers from the very symmetry of her being is a 'lady,' or better still, a 'noble woman.' "[1]

These women had an advantage over many women of their day, for basic to their religious tenets was the idea of eternal growth and learning. "The glory of God is intelligence," the Prophet Joseph had taught them. But the dictates of tradition hindered these women, as others, from full development of their intellectual powers. As they exchanged ideas in the *Exponent*, they lamented the fact that all too often if a woman "attempts to advance in the scale of practical education any higher than to have an understanding of how to knit and sew, or scrub and cook, she is growing 'strong minded,' and that is 'awful.' "[2]

This very restriction on women, they felt, was one of the contributing factors to the unhappy state the world was in. As one sister put it:

---

[1]*Woman's Exponent,* 1 (December 15, 1872), 110.
[2]*Woman's Exponent,* 1 (May 15, 1873), 187.

Knowledge, when rightly used, hurts no one. No wonder society in the world is in such a condition, when mothers, the teachers and molders of the infant mind, are only to know those things that men think proper. Woman's duties in this life are trying and arduous. She should have the wisdom of a sage and be gentle as a dove. . . . Let woman have a practical education in all the departments of her life, and rise with a fixed determination to break the shackles that have so long bound her sex, and become free, as God made her to be, man's helpmeet and not his slave. Mothers should early impress these true facts upon the minds of their children, and instead of encouraging their boys in false notions, show them the inconsistency of one sex being held so superior to the other, where both are born of the same parents. We trust there is a new era opened up for women. Noble is her work and great her responsibility.[3]

This same feeling was expressed by Eliza R. Snow:

In our past, how limited has been the educational advantages of woman! Book-learning was supposed to have very little to do with the requisite acquirements of the ideal housekeeper; the masses really believing that "woman should understand only sufficient Geography to know the different apartments in her house, and enough Chemistry to keep the kettle boiling." How absurd! If "knowledge is power" why should not woman possess her full quota as well as the sterner sex? She who is entrusted with the sacred responsibility of bearing the souls of men, of ministering to the wants and necessities of her household. Is it not she who must furnish their nutriment, not only to the new-born infant, but 'tis she who must supply the ever-recurring demands of the older and stronger members of the family. Truly the most thorough housekeepers, the best wives and mothers, are those who are best educated.[4]

The leading brethren of the Mormon Church were also encouraging education for women. Not only Brigham Young but later prophets held this philosophy. Joseph F. Smith in 1891 told the young women of the Church:

Seek to be educated in the highest meaning of the term; get the most possible service out of your time, your body and

[3]Mary Jane Crosby, "Woman's Position," *Woman's Exponent,* 9 (August 15, 1880), 49.

[4]E. R. S. [Eliza R. Snow], "Practical Education," *Woman's Exponent,* 11 (September 15, 1882), 61.

brains, and let all your efforts be directed into honorable channels, that no effort shall be wasted, and no labor result in loss or evil.[5]

The great crime of letting young women face the adult responsibilities of family life or other of the world's challenges with a mind that was not equipped was a theme to which Mormon women often addressed themselves. Representative of their comments are these:

A striking feature of the new woman is her willingness to learn. She feels that her safety is in a broad education, and she educates herself, if she has been unable to take the training of college and travel. She is not afraid to study physiology thoroughly and know the facts of life. With a knowledge of the delicate poise of mind and body, she can understand herself better and be infinitely better prepared to face the world than the old-fashioned girl of sweet sixteen with her baby-face and, alas, too often, the baby mind. Ignorance is not innocence. On the other hand knowledge is not power unless it be combined with wisdom. The new woman, then, would be wise.[6]

There is nothing so pitiful as the marriage of young, ignorant people with childish minds. A friend of ours brought his fifteen-year-old daughter to our city to attend the high school. He said he didn't want her to go to the country high school back home. She would be just like all the other country girls, think she must get married at sixteen or seventeen. He wanted her to have some mental training, mix with girls whose mothers all believed in watching them carefully, in giving them sane standards and in giving them an education so enjoyable they would not want to be married too early. He said he would be glad even to have his daughter earn her living for a year or two before marriage, so that she needn't feel absolutely dependent on any man's pocket book.[7]

Much of the education that these women sought after was of necessity the informal kind. But inasmuch as it was

[5]"Our Girls' Department," *Young Woman's Journal*, 3 (December 1891), 143. Speech quoted is by Joseph F. Smith.
[6]Clara Nuttal, "The New Woman," *Young Woman's Journal*, 8 (March 1897), 281.
[7]Agnes Bostonne, "A Mother's Success Depends on Her Daughters," *Relief Society Magazine*, 13 (May 1926), 231.

Maud May Babcock (1867-1954), educator, actress, theatre director, first woman to preside over a board of trustees of a state educational institution. (*Courtesy of Utah State Historical Society.*)

Alice Louise Reynolds (1873-1938), first woman to teach academic subjects at Brigham Young University, writer, public speaker, active in politics and women's clubs. (*Courtesy of Utah State Historical Society.*)

possible they took advantage of opportunities for formal training. Not many years before, women were barred from higher education. Concerning the opening of this area to women an editorial appeared in the *Relief Society Magazine,* written by Alice Louise Reynolds, who was the first woman to teach college subjects other than needlework, cooking, and music at Brigham Young University. Miss Reynolds recalled the beginnings of women in higher education in these words:

> Oberlin College, in the State of Ohio has the unique distinction of being the first college in the United States to open its doors to women on equal footing with men. One of the first women to take advantage of this then very extraordinary occurrence was Miss Lucy Stone, afterwards widely known as Lucy Stone Blackwell. In course of time she was graduated from the college. During her last year at Oberlin, she wrote a paper that excited the admiration of the faculty. They were proud of her achievement, and wished very much to have it read at the commencement exercises, but, being wholly unused to the thought of a woman on the platform, they tried to arrange to have it read by one of their own number. When Miss Stone became acquainted with the plan, she protested the injustice of the whole affair, saying that if she was to be denied the privilege of reading her own paper, she would not consent to its being read by anyone else.
>
> Some time after this event, Miss Stone was invited to deliver the commencement address at Oberlin College. She was asked while there how she felt the movement for the emancipation of women was progressing, and she replied, "It is certainly making progress, for when I first began campaigning for women's rights," and Miss Stone always emphasized the educational phase of her subject, "it was customary to throw rotten eggs at me; now at least the eggs that are hurled are fresh eggs." . . . Great as has been the advance made by women in higher education, we feel that it is the future that is big with promise.[8]

An observation of the national scene concerning women in higher education in 1880 gave this picture:

> The rusty hinges of Harvard College are slowly creaking to admit women to the same course of study, but not the same

---

[8]Alice Louise Reynolds, "Women and Higher Education," *Relief Society Magazine,* 10 (October 1923), 492, 493.

honors; the young lady students are not to be called students, and are not to use the college library, or be admitted to competitive honors, and not entitled to diplomas when the course is finished. Here is a bit of fossilized wisdom worthy to be remembered.[9]

But things seemed to be more promising at home. It was in 1850, just three years after the first migration to Utah, that the legislature passed a law establishing the first university west of the Missouri river, existing today as the University of Utah. Later, Church academies sprang up, similar to public high schools. The first of these, established in 1875, developed into what is now Brigham Young University at Provo. By 1911 there were twenty-two Mormon academies in the Rocky Mountain states. All of these both men and women were encouraged to attend.

That the education of girls was taken seriously at these institutions is attested by the remarks of one of the outstanding professors who taught at BYU, L. John Nuttall:

> Now, girls, just as all other civilized human beings, love to learn, and they love to learn because when God made them He put into the hearts and into the minds of every one of them an instinct that we call curiosity. . . .
>
> There is not very much difference between boys and girls when you come to teach them. There is the same interest, the same inspiration coming from seeing them grow, the same human desires, and the same things to be loved. . . . Girls can think just as acutely and just as deeply, just as fundamentally, and they like to do it, just as well as boys do, so that they are all alike in this one particular trait. . . .
>
> You cannot keep girls interested today unless you let them think. They will think in spite of you, because that is the spirit of the times. . . . We are getting away from that dependent, silent submission on the part of our girls, and they are as aggressive as Puritan Priscilla, and are making their own social life much more actively than they have ever done before. I am sure that this is not bad. I am sure it is in harmony with our fundamental thought. The girl of today is thinking, and thinking she is going to direct her own actions according to her thoughts,

---

[9]"An Address," *Woman's Exponent,* 8 (February 15, 1880), 143.

68   *The Flight and the Nest*

and if we are going to teach her along this line we must teach
her on the level of her intellect, as well as on the level of the
emotional appeal. The girls today must be given facts.[10]

Many of the pioneer Mormon women made great sacri-
fices in order to obtain an education, some of them being
specifically called by Brigham Young to go East and study
the subject of medicine. Throughout their writings is a feeling
of admiration for women both inside and outside of Mormondom who succeeded against all odds in obtaining an education.

A small note in the "Happenings" column of the *Relief
Society Magazine* in 1932 tells us that "Edna Searcy, age
17, of Louisiana, having heard that produce in lieu of cash
would be accepted in tuition at the State University, appeared
on the campus one day driving nine head of cattle. She was
admitted to the University all right."[11] Education was worth
the sacrifice.

But certainly not all the women of the pioneer era could,
or perhaps wanted to, engage in formal education. There
were other ways to cultivate the mind, and these they constantly recommended to one another. The weekly Relief
Society lessons gave them capsule acquaintanceships with
history, philosophy, social service, health, literature, art, geography, and a wide variety of other subjects. Self-education
was available to all, and they were encouraged to use it. An
essay in the *Exponent* in 1880 tells the benefits of reading:

> A good book is to the mind what wholesome food is to
> the body — it strengthens life and gives food for reflection. . . .
> I often hear ladies say they cannot take periodicals for they have
> no time to read. That is wrong. They have no right to starve
> themselves in such a way. How can they do their duty as wives
> and mothers if they encase themselves in a shell of ignorance?
> They may pass their lives in labor and care, their children may
> be the cleanest, and their homes the neatest, or they may pass

[10]L. John Nuttall, "The Teacher of Girls," *Young Woman's Journal,* 34
(August 1928), 420-426.

[11]Annie Wells Cannon, "Happenings," *Relief Society Magazine,* 19 (December 1932), 729.

it in crimping their hair and ruffling their dresses. What matters it? These things please the eye, but they pass away, and what remains?

They fill the measure of their lives in a degree, and pass off, and who shall rise up to call them blessed? True, they have toiled and drudged, they have given of their strength to the uplifting of their burdens; but have they given of their capacity if they have failed to cultivate their intelligence?

How shall they learn of the beautiful things of life if they know nothing beyond the gossip of the neighborhood; and knowing so little, how shall they impart wisdom to their children, or train them for the higher purposes of life? "How," says one, "shall a woman with little children in her arms, and the duties of life pressing upon her, find time to read?" She may not read lengthy or monotonous works in a comprehensive manner, for when the body is weary the mind is weak and cannot concentrate its powers to understand scientific treatises or works of magnitude. She cannot be benefited by that which requires profound thought or deep study. But that is no reason why a woman should not read. . . .

There are those, no doubt, having plenty of time for instructive reading, who spend it foolishly, who fritter away the precious moments of life, which are given them for a better purpose, in pampering pride and frivolity. Their labors are unsatisfactory, and when age shall come upon them they will have no store of knowledge to comfort their declining years. Reading alone should not engross our time; there are many things in practical life that demand our attention, many things necessary to study in the laws of progression. We should try to keep up with the times in which we live that we may be interesting and instructive companions to our young people. In that way we can best get an influence over their minds to guard them from the follies and temptations that surround them.

A mother has no right to consider her duties done when her children can attend to their personal wants. She must cultivate her mind that she may be enabled to lead them on, lest they, in their "higher education," go out of her depth and elude her grasp.

To do this it is necessary to mingle somewhat in society, that she may know what kind of company her children are keeping and how to regulate their manners and habits. She should take pains to have her mind well informed that she may be able to instruct and entertain them. It will give them a higher estimate of their parents in a social point of view, and lead them to more harmonious relations in life.[12]

One was never too busy, or too old, to cultivate herself intellectually. After all, had not Julia Ward Howe learned Greek after she was fifty years old?[13]

The results of their feelings about education, to me, are evident. Those women who speak from the pages of the early periodicals of the Mormon women are well-read, bright, courageous in subject and in style, articulate, and have a facility with idea and word that women of today might well envy.

So there they were — struggling with the hardships of pioneer life, making the desert blossom as the rose, raising large families, milking, churning, quilting, planting, and reaping — and still yearning for, and often accomplishing, remarkable cultivation of the mind. Some things, they knew, were temporal; others were eternal. Life was short, and some things must be placed before others. One sister versified:

> Bessie, don't be counting cobwebs.
>   Why, when you are laid to rest,
> Gossips will be searching corners
>   For the things that please them best.
> If it's cobwebs, they will find them.
>   If it's virtues sweet and rare
> That a dearest friend would mention,
>   They will find such virtues there.
> You're a thrifty little housewife,
>   But you labor quite in vain,
> If, with all your anxious sweeping,
>   Cobwebs gather on your brain.[14]

[12]Mary, "Pipsey Papers — No. 11," *Woman's Exponent,* 8 (March 1, 1880), 151.

[13]*Woman's Exponent,* 10 (April 15, 1882), 170.

[14]Annie D. S. Palmer, "Cobwebs," *Relief Society Magazine,* 3 (January 1916), 16.

CHAPTER 7

And Have Dominion

On the very first page of the very first issue of the *Woman's Exponent* in 1872 appeared this comment:

> Reverend James Freeman Clark claims "that if it is an advantage to vote, women ought to have it; if a disadvantage men ought not to be obliged to bear it alone." Speaking from experience we feel safe in affirming that the Reverend gentleman is right.[1]

The question of suffrage and other questions of political participation continued to play an important part in the writings of Mormon women for many decades.

And they did indeed speak from experience. Universal religious suffrage existed in the Church from the time of the restoration. "All things shall be done by common consent in the Church . . . ,"[2] and women voted along with men on the approval of church officers and the acceptance of revelations. And in February 1870 the territorial legislature of Utah passed a statute permitting women to vote. Wyoming had passed such a statute the year before, but because of the scheduling of elections the first female citizens in the nation to vote in a regular United States election were the Mormon women of Utah.[3]

---

[1]*Woman's Exponent*, 1 (June 1, 1872), 1.
[2]D & C 26:2.
[3]Leonard J. Arrington, "Blessed Damozels: Women in Mormon History," *Dialogue*, 6 (Summer 1971), 30.

The women were very pleased with this move and were determined that women throughout the entire country should share the benefits. On February 19, just seven days after the passage of their bill, and two days before the exercise of their vote for the first time, the minutes of a general meeting of the Female Relief Society in Salt Lake City record that Eliza R. Snow laid an item of business before the meeting, suggesting that "Sister Bathsheba W. Smith be appointed on a mission to preach retrenchment all through the South, and woman's rights, if she wished." The suggestion was acted upon.[4]

In 1887 the Edmunds-Tucker Act prohibited the women of Utah from voting, and the privilege was not restored until 1896. During the time when they could vote and the time when they couldn't, Mormon women continued to work very hard for an assured national suffrage. It was a long and difficult battle against prejudice and the conditioning of centuries. Many of the arguments used against female suffrage appear incredible now that years have passed and things can be seen in better perspective. One Mormon woman, Alice Louise Reynolds, who lobbied with a number of senators prior to the passage of the amendment, recalled that an anti-suffragist senator from Georgia said to her:

> "You have suffrage in Utah, haven't you, Miss Reynolds?" When she replied in the affirmative, he said, "Well, you go home and enjoy it. We don't want it in Georgia. We have a toast we drink to Georgia women that we don't want to change. We never wish to drink to the toast 'women once our superiors and now our equals.'"[5]

The argument that women were too good to participate in the mire of politics — that such activities as voting would degrade them — was the subject of a poem my grandmother, Sarah Oakey Sirrine, used to perform at suffrage meetings in Dingle Dell, Idaho. No one in the family has a copy of

---

[4]Edward W. Tullidge, *The Women of Mormondom* (New York: 1877), p. 501.

[5]Amy Brown Lyman, *A Lighter of Lamps, The Life Story of Alice Louise Reynolds* (Provo, Utah: The Alice Louise Reynolds Club, 1947), p. 52.

it, but Aunt Mamie recalls its general content. Marindy's husband is instructing her that she is too good to get mixed up in such business as voting. "No, Marindy, you're not going to go down to those dirty, filthy polls. No, not my Marindy." And after further extolling of her delicacy and refinement which he will not allow to be polluted, the husband concludes, "Now, Marindy, get out there and feed those pigs and load that hay!" According to Aunt Mamie, this presentation always brought down the house.

Suffrage meetings were held often, and information concerning national suffrage meetings was made available in the *Exponent*. The following note appeared in May 1880, signed by Susan B. Anthony:

> A mass meeting for all women who want to vote, will be held at Farwell Hall 148 Madison St., between Clark and La-Salle Street, Chicago, Ill., Wednesday, June 2d, 1880, at 10 a.m., 2.30 and 8 p.m.
>
> Every woman in the United States who sees or hears of this call is most earnestly invited to be present at this meeting. If this is impossible, she is urged to send a letter or postal, with her name and wish expressed in her briefest and strongest manner.[6]

Their own local meetings featured discussions, speeches, and songs. A *Utah Woman Suffrage Song Book,* priced at ten cents, was published and distributed by the *Exponent* around 1880. It included twenty songs, most of them with original lyrics by Utah women to be sung to existing tunes. Representative of these is one by the first editor of the *Exponent,* Louisa Lulu Greene Richards. It is entitled "Woman, Arise," and is sung to the tune of "Hope of Israel":

> Freedom's daughter, rouse from slumber;
> See, the curtains are withdrawn
> Which so long thy mind hath shrouded;
> Lo! thy day begins to dawn.

---

[6]"A Mass Meeting," *Woman's Exponent,* 8 (May 1, 1880), 182.

Chorus:
Woman, 'rise, thy penance o'er,
Sit thou in the dust no more;
Seize the scepter, hold the van,
Equal with thy brother, man.

Truth and virtue be thy motto,
   Temp'rance, liberty and peace,
Light shall shine and darkness vanish,
   Love shall reign, oppression cease.

Chorus: Woman, 'rise, etc.

First to fall 'mid Eden's bowers,
   Through long suff'ring worthy proved,
With the foremost claim thy pardon,
   When earth's curse shall be removed.

Chorus: Woman, 'rise, etc.[7]

The president of the Church, Joseph F. Smith, was invited
to one of these meetings, not knowing until after he arrived
that it was a meeting called in the interest of woman suffrage.
He spoke to the sisters, and the general contents of his speech
were recorded in the minutes:

He was in favor of woman suffrage, and that women should
enjoy all the privileges and rights that the men enjoyed; but he
was not so ardent an advocate for women to fill every and all
of the offices which men filled, as some others might be. . . .
He thought there were some offices in civil government. . . . re-
quiring physical endurance and exposures, exertions and strength
and other qualities, for which men were better fitted physically and
mentally than women. . . .

He thought the women were making a mistake in asking
too much at once — not that they should not have all that belonged to them, or of right they should have, but there were so
many things embraced in the women's right movement that
seemed formidable to many, very many men, and also objection-
able to them, that opposition to the whole movement was the
result. If the women would confine their efforts to woman suffrage
and that alone until they got it, they would have power in their

[7]*Utah Woman Suffrage Song Book* (Salt Lake City: n.p., n.d.), pp. 5, 6.

hands to further contend for and claim their privileges. . . . to make themselves heard and heeded, and . . . go on to perfection.[8]

Contending that "suffrage is neither a manly act nor yet a womanly act, but the act of a human being, who, as part of the people, has an inherent right to express or refuse consent to the form of government under which he or she lives,"[9] the Mormon women continued to exert distinguished service, working locally, attending national conventions, writing to legislators, lobbying, waiting, and praying.

In October 1920 the *Young Woman's Journal* carried these words:

> On August 26th this message flashed across the wires: "At eight o'clock this morning, in the presence of a notable gathering of suffragists who viewed the proceedings with eager interest, Secretary Colby signed the national proclamation enfranchising 27,000,000 women qualified to vote in America."[10]

The companion publication, the *Relief Society Magazine,* said concerning this event, "Of necessity there was much sacrifice, much humiliation, and much fatigue along the way; but it was a glorious struggle, and glorious has been its consummation."[11]

At the time of the passage of the "Susan B. Anthony Amendment," the women of Utah, led by Emily Sophia Tanner Richards, held a "victory meeting" at the state capitol, where the most ardent workers, among them Emmeline B. Wells, far advanced in years, "mingled their voices in thankful praise for the victorious end of the struggle." Mrs. Richards became the leader of the Utah delegation to the National Suffrage Victory Celebration, attended by women from throughout the nation.[12]

---

[8]"Speech of President Joseph F. Smith," *Salt Lake Stake Relief Society Record 1880-1892,* pp. 186-188, Church Archives.

[9]L. L. D. [Lucinda Lee Dalton] *Woman's Exponent,* 8 (January 15, 1880), 122.

[10]"The Suffrage Victory for Women in the United States," *Young Woman's Journal,* 31 (October 1920), 569.

[11]"Ten Years of Suffrage," *Relief Society Magazine,* 17 (May 1930), 242.

[12]*In Memoriam: Emily Sophia Tanner Richards,* p. 19.

The obtaining of the ballot was but the first step in moving into the area of politics and public service. The right to hold public office was not included in the initial statute that gave Utah women the right to vote; but it was a privilege that they soon asked for. The pages of the *Exponent* in 1880 let us know that a "Woman's Bill," permitting females the right to hold office, was being considered by the legislature; and the women were actively campaigning in its behalf. Of course, prejudice and tradition accompanied the struggle. One sister wrote in a letter to Emmeline B. Wells:

> We have been very successful here. All the principal gentlemen in the place have signed the petition, the Mormon brethren with only one or two exceptions. One very "knowing man," refused, expressing his views on woman's rights in this manner: "All the rights a woman needs is the right to a good husband." Wonderful wisdom![13]

Another reported:

> A prominent gentleman admitted he had declared publicly that "no pure and virtuous woman would wish to hold a political office," and said he would yet say he did "not believe God ever intended a woman to hold an office." I thought, what of Miriam, the prophetess? Why did not the great prophet and leader, Moses, cut down her ambition? And could both he and Aaron have been duped by a woman, men of God as they were? Was Deborah, the judge, a pure and virtuous woman? The Bible does not record that the court atmosphere polluted her fame.[14]

In responding to a gentleman's argument that woman should have no jurisdiction in public life because in the home she reigns supreme, and ought to, one sister wrote to the *Exponent*:

> Speaking of woman's sphere being "within the sacred precincts of home," he says: "There she reigns supreme, and she ought to." This exceedingly radical statement must be divided into two heads for greater ease of decapitation:

---

[13]*Woman's Exponent*, 8 (February 15, 1880), 141.
[14]"Items," *Woman's Exponent*, 8 (February 15, 1880), 142.

First — "There she reigns supreme." If this were true, so that men and not women were thus conquered singly, I submit that the aggregate of power would be in our hands and we certainly could not petition our subjects (and get refused) for terms of equality. Moreover, since it really is equality and not supremacy which we desire, no just and reasonable woman wishes to reign supreme at home or elsewhere. She wants an equal voice in family affairs, and an equal ownership in children and purse. So far from this being the case, the man by law has always been the sole dictator and proprietor, not only of policy, children and property, but of the woman herself included. Wonderful supremacy this! So off goes the first head.

Second — "And she ought to." Now, I protest that here is more granted — say, thrust upon us — than the strongest minded woman, or the one of most "nerve," ever dreamed of asking. Now, if we dared accept this oracle of "Vidi," what would become of St. Paul's time-honored advice, "Wives submit," &c., or what of those fearful things lately quoted to us concerning "women rule over them, and children are their oppressors?" These things are brought up by those who fear to allow any woman to hold an office, lest she should thus sin against conscience and scripture by ruling over people. Now, from a distance this looks like a large-sized bugaboo, but calm your fears, "mes enfants," and see how frail it is. No doubt you have all heard delegates elect make their farewell address to their constituents, and not one of them ever failed to assure the sovereign people that "I go, not your ruler, but your servant, subject to your orders and bound to obey your instructions." So you see that according to men's own definition of such a position, those who believe in woman's subserviency ought to be anxious to send her to the Legislature. But off with this second head, for in the Ideal Society we will all serve each other; and we deny that a woman — or a man — ought to reign supreme at home, or anywhere else. Let us all be free and equal.[15]

Another sister, writing from Manti, put it this way:

Many of our opponents seem to think if the Woman's Bill eventually becomes a law that all women, regardless of home duties or qualifications for office, will speedily degenerate into that most contemptible class of God's creatures, office seekers.

---

[15]"Not Dead, But Sleepeth," *Woman's Exponent,* 8 (March 15, 1880), 158, 159.

Now, from my knowledge of our virtues and their aims and purposes, a greater fallacy does not exist. Certainly not one woman in a hundred can leave her home to perform the duties pertaining to any public office. Probably a less proportion have any inclination in that direction. But we wish to feel that we have the right to hold positions of public trust where we are mentally and morally capable and when we represent the will of a majority of our fellow citizens.

In short we have grown tired, as Mrs. Stanton pertinently remarks, of being classed with idiots, lunatics and criminals. It is true we have the right of suffrage, but is this all, this shadow without the substance, that our brethren can afford to give us, the women of Utah, co-workers with them in the redemption of Zion and the upbuilding of the kingdom of the Latter days? . Nevertheless we feel and believe that our cause will eventually prevail and in that day we shall be proud to remember and do honor to our gallant defenders.[16]

The bill was indeed passed by the legislature, but then was vetoed by Governor Axtell. The women continued, however, to work for the privilege of holding public office. And many of their "gallant defenders" were men, one of whom, a gentleman from American Fork, wrote a lengthy essay in the *Exponent,* entitled "Woman in Politics," which makes some interesting points. His first paragraph tells us, "I will speak of woman as a factor in governmental affairs." He then continues:

All agree the terms "man," "mankind" mean women as well as men, in religion, science, literature and song. . . . On one point, however, we do not see eye to eye, and that is in the high, towering domain of politics. Here we enter upon holy ground, here we must take off our shoes and tread lightly, here we must drop half the brains and half the heart of the nation; for in political lingo "man," "men" means exclusively the "lords of creation." And as a necessary corollary governments derive their just powers from the consent of the masculine gender, and women have no rights politically that the house of lords are bound to respect. Words rightly interpreted, however, in politics, as well as religion, give woman her just rights, and when things are done by common consent, she is included as a party to the transaction. When the Savior says He will draw all men unto

[16]"Equal Rights," *Woman's Exponent,* 8 (March 1, 1880), 146.

him, "he who believeth and is baptized shall be saved" — and Paul — "God wills all men to be saved." Do they mean exclusively men? I think not. Else Paul made a mistake when he said, "the man is not without the woman in the Lord."

A monarchy may prescribe woman in her rights, and perhaps survive, but a republic cannot afford to let half its intellect and morality lie fallow. Her assistance is needed in public affairs. . . . I hold that neither sex alone is competent to rightly control the political destiny of the whole. It is by uniting them that the best results are obtained. God intended man and woman to supplement each other, and no system of government can be perfect till the divine theory is carried out. The caucus must be elevated by the introduction of women, to the equality of the parlor. Society, with its culture and refinement, is always above politics in its moral tone. The world is full of examples illustrative of the refining influence of one sex upon the other. Half a dozen girls will rescue a whole university from rowdyism, while a few boys are sufficient to train a girls' school to refinement. This law of mutual restraint and influence is general, and politics must be brought within the sphere of its operation if we would purify the political atmosphere. . . .

In the foregoing observations the following are made to appear. The natural equality of man including woman. The right of the majority to govern. Their duty so to govern as to preserve inviolate the sacred obligations of equal justice. That politically things are done by common consent. That governments derive their just powers from the consent of the governed. . . . That privileged classes or partial education, while portions are kept in ignorance, is not conducive to union nor strength. That the practice as well as the theory of government needs to be enjoyed by the people. That woman as well as man is under God the arbiter of her own destiny. That constitutions nor laws can rightfully discriminate because of sex; and that the field of politics as well as science, art, literature and the professions is open to man and woman. And in fact in all the relations and duties of life, woman should be side by side, a co-worker with, and helpmate for man. They belong to the same great family and their interests are identical and mutual.[17]

When Utah was admitted as a state in 1896, the state constitution provided for woman suffrage and also for woman's right to hold political office. An interesting event occurred

---

[17]L. E. H., "Woman In Politics," *Woman's Exponent*, 11 (July 1, 1882), 17, 18.

in the first election that followed. Angus Cannon was selected
as a candidate for the Republican party for the Utah State
Senate. His wife, Mattie Hughes Cannon, was petitioned
and agreed to stand as one of the Democratic candidates. Mrs.
Cannon was a bright and intellectual woman, who had studied
medicine under Dr. Romania B. Pratt in Salt Lake City, then
graduated from the University of Michigan, received an M.D.
degree from the University of Pennsylvania, and another
degree from the National School of Elocution and Oratory
in Philadelphia. Returning to Salt Lake City, she accepted
an appointment as resident physician at the Deseret Hospital.
In the election, she received 11,413 votes to her husband's
8,742.[18]

The *Relief Society Magazine* later said of the event:

> This political victory for Dr. Cannon had greater significance
> than appeared at the time. For everywhere in those days Mormon
> women were looked upon as nothing less than serfs, and this
> victory at the polls for a woman — a victory that could not have
> been won in any other State in the Union — really opened the
> eyes of the nation to the true state of affairs in Utah, so far
> as the women were concerned. A man and his wife running on
> opposite tickets, the man being a high ecclesiast in the dominant
> church, and the wife winning in a free vote of the people, most
> of whom were members of that church! It was a fact sufficient
> to astound the nation — which it did.
>
> Martha Hughes Cannon, therefore, was the first woman to
> become State senator, not only in Utah, but in the United States
> as well.[19]

Mormon women established other records in the field
of public service. As recalled in an address by President N.
Eldon Tanner, "Utah women were the first to achieve in many
civic fields. They were among the first to serve on juries, as
superintendents of public instruction, on boards of trustees
of state coeducational institutions, and as delegates to national
conventions."[20] And one of the first women mayors in the

---

[18]Arrington, "Blessed Damozels: Women in Mormon History," p. 31.

[19]John Henry Evans, "Martha Hughes Cannon," *Relief Society Magazine,*
19 (October 1932), 587, 588.

[20]N. Eldon Tanner, General Conference, Relief Society, October 2, 1974,
Typewritten transcript, p. 4.

Martha Hughes Cannon, (1857-1932), first woman
in the nation to be elected a state senator. Also
qualified as a doctor of medicine. Shown here in
1899 with daughter Gwendolyn. *(Courtesy of Utah
State Historical Society.)*

United States, if not the first, was Sister Mary Howard, who was elected in Kanab, Utah, in 1912, with four other Mormon sisters who formed an all-woman city council.[21]

As the Mormon women began to move into these fields of public service and saw some of the fruits of it, they became even more convinced that their influence there was needed. In 1923 one contributor to the *Relief Society Magazine* reasoned:

> Besides being the homemaker, she must be a community and city maker as well. This is partly because her children are in the home only a comparatively short time and partly because of her obligations as a citizen and a voter. She must therefore see that there is a neighborhood, a community or city for them to go out into that shall offer as great protection as possible to their health and character. The neighbors' interests become her interests. A certain street needs cleaning, a rubbish heap should be removed, or there is sickness, perhaps some contagious disease, which calls for a friendly attitude and cooperation, particularly in the strict observance of the quarantine laws. She needs to know the source of the water supply, food and milk supply, sewage disposal, proper regulation of proper morals and an understanding of social legislation.[22]

The following year appeared an example of how a woman, with her particular insight into things which men were not ordinarily acquainted with, made a significant contribution:

> An incident in the recent history of Chicago is to the point. A movement for a five-million-dollar bond issue was launched. The men wanted the issue for the making of a zoological garden, and, in keeping with their desires, all the big papers of Chicago were supporting their project. A woman connected with the Chicago schools chanced to know that the room provided for the school children of that city was wholly inadequate. Consequently she suggested that a counter campaign be inaugurated for a five-million-dollar bond issue for the building of school houses, and that the slogan of the campaign be "Monkeys or Kids."

[21]Leonard J. Arrington, "Achievements of Latter-day Saint Women," *Improvement Era,* 73 (April 1970), 62.

[22]Lalene H. Hart, "Conservation of Time and Energy Within and Without the Home," *Relief Society Magazine,* 10 (July 1923), 346.

The school people had no opportunity for publicity through the daily papers, so that they had to be contented with such publicity as might be afforded apart from the press. They tagged people on the streets, had processions of the children, in which they carried banners setting forth their desires. The thing "took like wildfire." Everywhere, in the streets, on the cars, in the shops, everybody was asking everybody else, "Who are you for, monkeys or kids?"

Election day came. The issue for the school bond went over two to one, and the issue for the zoo was defeated two to one. Had there not been a woman in Chicago who knew the school situation, and in addition to that, knew how to make the school situation known to others, in all probability the children would have continued to suffer for housing, the bond issue would have been put over for the zoo, and the monkeys would have won the day.[23]

The progress of women in community and national affairs, their election to various offices, was noted approvingly in the various publications of the Mormon women. The youngest woman mayor in the nation, the number of women in the nation that held responsible public office, women governors being elected in Texas and Wyoming, biographies of current women in the Utah legislature — any newsworthy item concerning women in political life was recorded. "I am firmly convinced," wrote Amy Brown Lyman, a state legislator, counselor and later president in the Relief Society general presidency, "that any legislative body is benefited by the presence of good and able women."[24]

They anticipated even greater things for women in this area, recalling in 1933 that Alice Stone Blackwell, daughter of the pioneer suffragist Lucy Stone, wrote, "From the sewing circle to the President's Cabinet in 100 years, may sound like a dream but it is the probable achievement of the American woman."[25] And in that same year they observed that

[23]"The Woman's Idea," *Relief Society Magazine*, 11 (March 1924), 120, 121.

[24]Amy Brown Lyman, *In Retrospect* (Salt Lake City: General Board of Relief Society, 1945), p. 84.

[25]Annie Wells Cannon, "Happenings," *Relief Society Magazine*, 20 (March 1933), 155.

looking at the names of women holding responsible positions made it appear even probable that there might one day be a woman president of the United States.[26]

The idea of a female chief executive, considered incredible by most people in the days of woman's emancipation, was given serious consideration by Emmeline B. Wells in 1884. Mrs. Belva Lockwood had accepted the nomination of the Woman's National Rights party for the office of President of the United States. Of this event Mrs. Wells observed:

> No doubt Mrs. Lockwood is in many, perhaps most respects quite as capable of occupying the honored position of the Chief Executive of the nation, as many of those who have figured in that capacity. She is a woman of great ability and her brain is as clear and her reasoning as logical as that of a man; she talks not only as fast, but as well; her language is as good; she hits the nail on the head quite as often, and hits as hard; she is brave and fearless. But she is a woman. And that any woman should aspire to the position would be sufficient to condemn her in the estimation of the masses of people. Yet they are never weary of extolling Queen Victoria, and even go as far back as Elizabeth of England for an example of woman's greatness. Then why not a superior American woman, one manifestly just as capable of holding the reins of powers as Victoria. . . .

> Mrs. Lockwood shall have our best wishes for her success as a nominee for President, and we have no doubt as to her ability to preside over the affairs of the nation. She is fearless for what she deems right, and valiant for justice, and will maintain her position on any matter of importance with quite as much independence of character as any man. Her Washington life has initiated her into many knotty points in the political issues now pending in Congress and she is, by means of her intuitive tact and grand opportunities, pretty well acquainted with the general business of the departments of state. In her manner she has the appearance of a military officer of high rank. She is certainly a woman of superior endowments and attainments, and if a woman were eligible to be President of the United States, there could be no good reason why it should not be Belva A. Lockwood.

---

[26]Annie Wells Cannon, "Happenings," *Relief Society Magazine,* 20 (June 1933), 357.

At any rate it is something to record the nomination of a woman for a position that has been always filled by a man. But times and things are changing and woman's hour is near, and Mrs. Lockwood does but anticipate, like some others, living too near the future; she feels the spirit of progress that is revolutionizing the old and breaking in pieces the iron rules of tradition and crumbling to atoms the theories of statesmen of olden times. A new era is being ushered in and women are born with hearts as large, and aims as lofty, and courage as undaunted as men — women who do their own thinking and who are not content to sit and dream and wait for the good time coming, but who will themselves open up the way for the advancement of others and thrust the sickle into the field of ripened grain. They may be called innovators and extremists, but, nevertheless, they will stand out grandly in the future and be applauded as benefactors of the human race, for what lifts woman elevates man, for is she not the mother of mankind? Mrs. Lockwood's nomination will, we ardently hope, call out expressions of sentiment and opinions upon the woman suffrage question that will eventually result in great good to the cause and enlighten a class of people who "sit in gross darkness" on this very important subject, one which in its bearing connects itself materially with that of many vital matters that stem up the tide of human progress and advancement.[27]

Participation in civic and governmental affairs appeared to the Mormon women an important part of their "flight." Not that they would substitute it for their nests, but they believed it could contribute to the well-being of those nests; and when the nests no longer demanded their presence as much they could then give fuller, significant public service. Their part in the dominion had been requested, worked for, made possible, and advanced toward.

[27]"Mrs. Lockwood's Nomination," *Woman's Exponent*, 13 (September 1884), 60.

CHAPTER 8

Wise Stewards

In 1882 the Mormon women read in the *Exponent* the following note:

> A woman dentist at Quebec has been denounced by the press for pursuing an unwomanly avocation, and the clergy of two parishes have prohibited their people from having anything to do with her.[1]

This must have sounded strange to the women of Deseret, whose own clergy, in the person of President Brigham Young, had made such comments as this:

> We believe that women are useful, not only to sweep houses, wash dishes, make beds, and raise babies, but that they should stand behind the counter, study law or physics, or become good bookkeepers and be able to do the business in any counting house, and all this to enlarge their sphere of usefulness for the benefit of society at large. In following these things they but answer the design of their creation.[2]

And it was a full ten years previously, in the very first issue of the *Exponent,* that Eliza R. Snow had written that there were many rights which women were denied by custom

---

[1]"Notes and News," *Woman's Exponent,* 11 (September 1, 1882), 49.

[2]John A. Widtsoe, ed., *Discourses of Brigham Young* (Salt Lake City: Deseret Book, 1973), pp. 216, 217.

and by statute law, and that among these rights was that each woman should have "access to every avenue of employment for which she has physical and mental capacity."[3]

Let us hasten to be assured that these women had not concluded it was necessary that every woman enter a prestigious profession, or hold a paying job, for most of her life. They felt that the position of homemaker was an honorable profession, that it contributed significantly to the nation's moral and economic well-being, and that no woman need be ashamed of giving all or most of her energies to that area. They felt, in fact, that the importance of being a good homemaker was underestimated, and that changes in society's thinking were necessary in order to bring it to a higher status. Toward this subject the *Exponent* printed a lengthy essay, taken from the *Englishwoman's Review,* entitled "Are Wives Supported?" Some of the points are well worth examining:

> Among the amusing paragraphs lately circulated in the variety column of newspapers is one which contains a deeper lesson than they can ordinarily boast of. "A husband advertised in the Sheffield *Daily Telegraph,* England, that he, Thomas A............, would no longer be answerable for the debts incurred by his wife. The wife retorted: 'This is to certify that I, Elizabeth A............, am able to pay my own debts, now that I have got shut of Tommy.'"
>
> This retort is a very pointed comment upon the theory that has prevailed up to the present day, namely, that the husband was the breadwinner and stay of the household, and that the subordinate members, including the wife and children, were supported by him, unprofitable members of the community, consumers instead of producers. . . . Are these women supported? Are they only consumers, or a most important section of the producers of the country's wealth? Do they do anything to earn their own living, and, if so, how can it be secured to them?
>
> A young man and woman agree to marry, and they bring into the joint partnership not real or personal property, inherited or acquired, but their heads and hands only. The man's head and hands are occupied out of doors; he is the visible wage-earner; he works ten or twelve hours and brings home enough,

[3]E., "Woman's Rights and Wrongs," *Woman's Exponent,* 1 (June 1, 1872), 5.

if he does not spend it at the public-house, to buy necessaries for the family. Perhaps by extra industry on his part, or extra good management on hers, he saves and puts by money. She, on her part, has kept a decent and comfortable home for him, has laid out his earnings for their mutual benefit, and has borne and brought up their family of children, and, as any one who has been in like circumstances will acknowledge, has worked not only through the day of twelve hours, but half the night also. She has labored in her own vocation as hard as he has; she has economised, contrived, schemed, saved, giving the whole of her time and brains to the common stock, and he has done no more. And yet the ordinary theory is that this woman is supported all her life. . . .

In many cases the unpaid partner of the domestic firm does more than the household work, though this seems a fair day's measure for any individual's brain or hands. If they keep a little shop, she looks after it; if a farm, she makes the butter, fattens the fowls, or feeds the calves. To quote again from the wisdom of the newspaper corners: "A Wester man having lost his wife, a sympathizing man remarked upon his woe-begone appearance. 'Well, I guess you would look thin too,' was the melancholy rejoinder, 'if you had to get up before daylight, make the fires, draw water, split wood, and feed the cattle before breakfast. I tell you what it is, if I don't get somebody to fill poor, dear, sainted Maria's place, I shall be resting by her side before many weeks.'" . . .

The labor of the household can only be performed free of cost when it is performed by the wife. Every one remembers Wilkie Collins' resumé of the question in the "Moonstone." The steward, whose cottage has been kept clean by a working woman, marries her, and says:

"I had another reason likewise of my own discovering. Selina, being a single woman, made me pay so much a week for her board and services. Selina, being my wife, couldn't charge for her board, and was bound to give me her services for nothing. That was the point of view I looked at it from. Economy — with a dash of love. I put it to my mistress as in duty bound, just as I had put it to myself. 'I have been turning Selina Goby over in my mind!' I said, 'and I think, my lady, it will be cheaper to marry her than to keep her!' . . ."

As we have endeavored to point out, the value of the work they do would be recognized at once had it to be paid for. Some well-intentioned but over-zealous reformers have suggested that

wives and mothers should receive regular wages from the husbands for the work they do. This, to our thinking, is manifestly
absurd and impossible. The work of caring for her family,
whether recognized as work or not, is the duty which she has
undertaken to do when she married. She is morally bound to
perform it, as much as the husband is morally bound to provide
her with the means of doing it. The sacred duties of wife and
mother are such as can be measured by no debtor or creditor
account. She and her husband have entered into a partnership, in
which each contributes his or her best for the good of the firm;
there can be no question of hire. . . .

A few words from a thoughtful article on "Treasurers," by
Colonel Higginson, in the *Woman's Journal* are to the point here:

"We are constantly told that the life work of a wife is as
arduous and absorbing as that of her husband. We are told
that if she does her whole duty to her family, she can have no
time to study metaphysics, or to put a slip of paper into a ballot-
box. I think it was the conservative, Dr. Edward H. Clark, who
declared that the duties of the mother of a family required as
much toil of brain and body as those of the captain of a ship.
Grant it all; grant that she work as hard as her husband does. If
so, the inference is irresistible that she earns her share of the
family income. The fact that he receives the money and pays
the bills makes him the treasurer of the family, that is all, and
he has no more right than any other treasurer to take airs upon
himself and talk nonsense. When he pays out money to her,
it is not as a gift, but as earnings."[4]

The Mormon women, then, were not advocating that
every woman go out and get a job. But they did feel that
every woman should be prepared to support herself, and this
for a number of reasons. One was the possibility of necessity.
As early as 1872 they printed this sentiment:

Nothing so tends to the degeneracy of womanhood as a life
of laziness and indulgence — an aim for a wealthy husband, and
then life with no object nor aim beyond raising a family. . . .
A very serious and common mistake in the training of our girls
is the neglect definitely to provide against the vicissitudes of life
with the faculty of noble self support. . . . Our girls . . . should
be made distinctly to understand that all the love romances lie,

and that there is no such thing as making a compact with fortune
to avert the necessity of honest toil. Nay, more, we would have
the girls taught that labor, especially brain labor, for the benefit
of the world, is too noble to be undertaken for mere mercenary
ends, albeit the world must and will pay for it.[5]

The same theme appears again and again. Fifty years
later in one of their lesson guides, the *Relief Society Magazine*
printed:

> Every girl should have ambition to qualify in two vocations
> — that of home making, and that of earning a living by other
> means whenever occasion requires. An unmarried woman is
> always happier when following a vocation in which she can be
> socially serviceable and financially independent. In no case
> should she be constrained to accept an unworthy companion
> as a means of support. Any married woman may become a
> widow at any time; property may vanish as readily as husbands
> may die. Thus any woman may be under the necessity of earn-
> ing her own living and helping to support dependents. Why should
> not she be trained for the duties and the emergencies of life?[6]

The fact that a woman has prepared herself to be self-
reliant and to fill a profession if circumstances require was
also seen as a point in her favor if and when she did marry.
A fictional story in the *Young Woman's Journal,* "The Maid
and Her Admirers," conveys this idea:

> Bessie found her school work more interesting each day
> and under the inspiring talks of the President developed an am-
> bition to work to some definite purpose.
>
> "Aunt Henry, I want to specialize," she announced one
> evening at dinner, "I'd like to take up some line of the world's
> work and succeed at it, as boys do. What would you suggest?"
>
> "Don't you expect to marry?" teased Mrs. Pinkhurst. She
> never would be serious at first.
>
> "In the dim, distant future, maybe; but that's on the lap of
> the gods," flounced the lassie with that independent lift of her
> small head which indicated a certain competency to take care of
> herself. "Meanwhile and whether or not, I intend to take up some

[5]*Woman's Exponent,* 1 (November 1, 1872), 83.
[6]*Relief Society Magazine,* 13 (April 1921), 249.

work and succeed at it, or at least — " she qualified — "I'm going to try to succeed."

"That's the way I like to hear girls talk," vowed Phil spiritedly. "I like to see them get in and accomplish things like we fellows do. Why shouldn't they?"

"Shouldn't they prepare themselves to be wives and mothers?" the Aunt threw out for the sake of argument.

"In a general way, yes, the same as we men prepare to be husbands and fathers," opined the boy. "But every girl should learn, also, to do some necessary labor that will make her economically independent. And the very fact that she has brains and industry sufficient to do something worthwhile is guarantee that she'll make a creditable wife and mother when those jobs show up."

Bessie enthusiastically applauded this speech for feminism as also did Mrs. Pinkhurst, showing her hand at last.[7]

Another reason the early Mormon women saw for a woman preparing herself to fill a vocation was that not all of her lifetime could possibly be completely filled with the demands of a home and children. The later years of a woman's life were viewed as a time that could be very socially and professionally productive. In an article called "Growing Old," reprinted from the *Woman's Journal* of San Francisco, the subscribers to the *Exponent* read:

> I have been thinking what a poor prospect the average woman has to look forward to, at the age of forty, if she be a widow without property.
>
> If she has raised a family of small children soon to be married and leave her, or if she be childless, the lookout is about the same. Her real life work seems done, when it ought to be only changed. The active matron cannot fold her hands, so she looks about for something to take up her time. What shall it be? Charity? General meddlesomeness? Shall she become a burden on step children?
>
> Happy the woman who has the foresight to see that through forty years of experience she has matured the ability to commence a grand, useful second half of her life! Let her study a profession

---

[7]Ida Stewart Peay, "The Maid and her Admirers," *Young Woman's Journal,* 29 (August 1918), 461.

or adopt a trade. The physician or lawyer with gray hairs has twice the practice he did during his probation of maturing experience and judgment.

It is the worry over the future that so wrinkles and ages women. They seem helpless, and, worst of all, not desired after a certain age. Every one should live young in ambition and work, no matter how many years they have seen roll by; each year should count a garnered store to make rich the coming one.

The first forty years of a woman's life are generally laid on the altar of love, and no pay taken in return. (I am not talking of the wealthy class.) The law gives a wife the poorest chance of any in life — housework without pecuniary pay. And when this situation is no longer open, she looks about, scared, for a place to earn her living. How many such have I seen; and I always advise them to acquire a trade, or a profession, or go to teaching. They make the best of teachers and are much to be preferred to younger tutors.

I would not advise any woman to leave unfinished family work; but when that is completed there is other grand work for her, if she has the courage to overcome objections.[8]

A similar plea is found in a statement by Dr. Elizabeth Chapin:

O mothers, do not fold the hands across your empty lap, and say at fifty, "The story is told." If home has been so all-absorbing that outside interests have fallen away from you, find the broken thread, or take up a new one, and you will soon find yourselves among the world's creators.[9]

The practical reasons were not the only ones advanced for the encouragement of women to equip themselves professionally. The world was in need of the exercise of gifts that had been placed within woman — certainly as they flowered through her children — but also as she herself might be able to give them. One sister wrote in 1880:

I am now fully convinced of woman's efficiency, not only as queen of the home circle, the "molder" of the minds of men, the guiding star of youth, the radiance of which can never be

---

[8]Beth, "Growing Old," *Woman's Exponent,* 9 (August 1, 1880), 38.
[9]"Miscellaneous," *Woman's Exponent,* 16 (June 15, 1887), 16.

eclipsed or rivaled by other lights. Nor do these immense boundaries limit her sphere. As I view the subject her influence for good extends far out into infinitude, her stopping place has not been designated, nor can the line of demarcation be drawn, especially now that the fiat has gone forth, and ere long will be heralded to all nations, calling earth's fair daughters in all the glory of their womanhood into the grand arena of science, art, literature, and *religion*. . . . Woman's hitherto dormant affinities will be called into activity, and she will display an efficient executive ability, that of itself will recommend her to offices of honor and trust.[10]

These lofty and generous concepts were, however, still to a large extent theoretical. Woman's boundaries, professionally, were rather fixed in those days. The following observation was made in 1913 by Annie Wells Cannon, president of the Pioneer Stake Relief Society and a member of the state legislature:

> Woman has always had one opportunity — the opportunity to work; this one thing has never been denied her. Man has never considered that she was out of her sphere when she toiled in the fields and factories; he has never criticized her for leaving her home for any kind of drudgery. But when she began to enter the professional field and when she began to compete with men in the great work of the world, she was reminded that she was going out of her own sphere and was neglecting her home.[11]

When Eliza R. Snow addressed this subject in the first issue of the *Exponent,* she pointed out that

> The needle and midnight candle are yet considered, by too many, the proper appliances of woman's sphere. Custom also says that if a woman does as much work as a man, and does it as well, she must not receive equal pay for it, and herein a wrong is inflicted upon her by the deprivation of a right to which she is justly entitled.[12]

A reason and possible remedy for this unfortunate situation was hinted at in a review of "Mrs. Duniway's Lecture."

---

[10]"A Sentiment," *Woman's Exponent,* 9 (July 15, 1880), 26.
[11]"General Relief Society Conference," *Woman's Exponent,* 41 (May 1913), 52.
[12]E., "Woman's Rights and Wrongs," p. 5.

Mrs. Duniway was "an able champion of human rights," whose only extreme was her "reverence for the sacred office of motherhood." As one sister recalled part of her address:

> She said that while it was her only ambition to be a good wife and mother, her husband missed his financial balance, and about the same time met with a personal injury, which drove her to the school room and thence to a millinery store. She competed disadvantageously with men. Around her were other women struggling similarly to keep their heads above water, and claiming her assistance.

> At the close of a day's labor in which sympathy and aid had been called in different directions, and disasters and snubs had been unusually prevalent, she approached the low couch on which her invalid husband was lying, and seating herself on the carpet laid her head against him. After rehearsing the difficulties of the day, she said, "Why are these things?" Her noble and generous husband (that is what she called him) said, "My dear, these things must in the nature of things be so until woman takes her proper position as the social and political equal of man." She said an inspiration seemed to enable her to comprehend that moment what she had heard him talk many times before.[13]

Despite the odds against the professional advancement of women, the sisters in Utah did some remarkable things. One event occurred in 1872 that hit the national press. *The Missouri Republican,* under the heading "The Oppressed Women of Utah," made the following comments:

> We have heard a good deal about the oppressed and degraded women of Utah. . . . This string has been tuned and played upon until it appears to have snapped. . . . They have more power and more rights than they have anywhere on this green earth. . . . An incident which calls up the privileges which the women of Utah enjoy, lately occurred in Salt Lake City. Miss Phoebe Couzens, of St. Louis, and Miss Georgie Snow, daughter of the Attorney-General of the Territory, were admitted to the bar in the District Court, and the ceremonies were imposing.[14]

---

[13]Rheuma, "Mrs. Duniway's Lecture," *Woman's Exponent,* 1 (July 15, 1872), 29.

[14]*Woman's Exponent,* 1 (October 15, 1872), 73.

Turning the page we discover that the first woman lawyer on the Pacific Coast was refused admission to the bar of Santa Cruz, California.[15] An editorial in the *Exponent,* called "Lady Lawyers," gave this sentiment:

> We recognize in the application and admission of these ladies a principle which is daily receiving wider recognition and which was, a few years ago, ridiculed when advocated by enlarged minds that looked beyond their time — the right of a woman to earn her living in any honorable career for which she has capacity. In the practical working of this principle, as in everything which aims at securing to woman the exercise of her full and legitimate rights, Utah has been markedly in advance of other parts of the Union. . . . In every direction in which woman's talents or powers can be made available, there is every encouragement for their cultivation and development.[16]

The medical profession was another area in which the Mormon women were making some significant strides. Brigham Young was of the mind that many of the medical needs of the communities could better be cared for by female doctors, and so he encouraged, and sometimes officially called, women to go East and study medicine. In 1873 Eliza R. Snow said to the women in Ogden at a Relief Society meeting:

> President Young wants a good many to get a classical education, and then get a degree for Medicine. . . . In ancient times we know that women officiated in this department, and why should it not be so now? . . . We have to get up these classes and attend to all these things. Don't you see that our sphere is increasing? Our sphere of action will continually widen, and no woman in Zion needs to mourn because her sphere is too narrow.[17]

This was thirty-four years after the first diploma as doctor of medicine was given to a woman, Elizabeth Blackwell. The same year that Eliza was stumping for female medical students, Romania B. Pratt (later Penrose) left to study in Philadelphia, coming home after graduating and

[15]*Ibid.,* p. 75.
[16]"Lady Lawyers," *Woman's Exponent,* 1 (October 1, 1872), 68.
[17]Eliza R. Snow, "Address," *Woman's Exponent,* 2 (July 15, 1873), 37.

serving an internship to serve as a specialist in eye surgery and in obstetrics.[18] She worked for the establishment of the Deseret Hospital, becoming its first resident physician. She was generous with her medical knowledge, encouraging women to learn and practice. In 1880 the readers of the *Exponent* were informed of a "Class in Midwifery — Dr. Romania B. Pratt will open a class in this branch of medicine in her office in the Constitution Building, on the 10th of May, at 4 p.m.[19]

The *Exponent* followed the careers of other female doctors, offering encouragement and congratulations. One of these was Mattie Paul Hughes (later Cannon, previously mentioned as the first woman state senator), whom the *Exponent* welcomed home in 1882 from an absence of four years' study, "preparing herself for a life of eminent usefulness."[20]

That same year, ten years after the invitation went out to the Mormon women, they prided themselves that some success had been achieved in entering this profession.

> With about half a dozen ladies who have graduated with honors, in the medical profession, and others now in some of the best colleges and universities in the United States, Utah may certainly make a fair showing of women doctors.[21]

These and other doctors produced by the Mormon women in the 1870s and 1880s are called by Church Historian Leonard J. Arrington "the most remarkable group of women doctors in American history."[22] To themselves they were remarkable for many reasons. When Sister Penrose, the first of their number, died in 1932, the *Relief Society Magazine* editorialized: "She proved that a woman can be a good homemaker, wife and mother, and at the same time do public work of the finest character."[23]

----

[18]Arrington, "Blessed Damozels: Women in Mormon History," p. 27.
[19]"Home Affairs," *Woman's Exponent,* 8 (May 1, 1880), 180.
[20]"A Young Lady Doctor," *Woman's Exponent,* 11 (August 1, 1882), 37.
[21]"Women Doctors," *Woman's Exponent,* 11 (July 15, 1882), 28.
[22]Arrington, "Blessed Damozels: Women in Mormon History," p. 27.
[23]Dr. Romania B. Penrose," *Relief Society Magazine,* 19 (December 1932), 740.

Romania B. Pratt Penrose (1839-1932), first woman
doctor and surgeon in Utah, first resident physician
of the Deseret Hospital, mother of seven children.
(Courtesy of Utah State Historical Society.)

In the field of literature the Mormon women were also active. The three periodicals issued by and for women, extensively quoted in this book, offered great opportunity for the women to express themselves in print. It is also impressive that in the 1870s and 1880s more than three dozen books of poetry, autobiography, and history were published by Latter-day Saint women.[24] Emmeline B. Wells detailed some of these books in a speech given in Chicago:

> Two volumes of poems by Eliza R. Snow were published at an early date, and later, after her travels in the Holy Land, *Correspondence of Palestine Tourists,* also books for children, etc., nine volumes in all.
>
> The poems of Sarah E. Carmichael, one of our Utah girls, have been so widely celebrated that William Cullen Bryant selected from her effusions for his edition of poets of America. She also published her poems in book form. Among the women who have been fortunate enough to bring out books of prose and verse are Augusta Joyce Crocheron, born in Boston, but reared in the West, who issued *Wild Flowers of Deseret, Representative Women of Deseret,* and one book for children; Hannah T. King, an English woman, born in Cambridge, issued three, *Songs of the Heart, Scripture Women,* and an Epic Poem; Mary J. Tanner, *Fugitive Poems,* Emily B. Spencer, from Connecticut, two volumes of poems, and several others, of which time fails one to tell.[25]

Sister Wells closed her remarks with the assurance that "it remains for the future to reveal the magnificent possibilities of song and story of the drama and romance from the gifted pens of the daughters of the valleys of the Rocky mountain fastnesses which lie by the inland sea."[26]

Utah also provided good ground for women to become professional educators. Susa Young Gates tells us that the first woman university president or principal was Miss Ida Ione Cook, who presided over the University of Utah from 1871 to 1873. She was also the first woman county super-

---

[24] Arrington, "Blessed Damozels: Women in Mormon History," p. 26.
[25] Emmeline B. Wells, "Emmeline B. Wells on Women Authors and Journalists," *Woman's Exponent,* 21 (June 15, 1893), 178.
[26] *Ibid.*

intendent of schools in the nation, serving for Cache County in that office from 1879 to 1880. Among other prominent educators was Maud May Babcock, who was the first woman to preside over a board of trustees of a state educational institution, serving twelve years as president of the board of the State School for the Deaf and Blind from 1905 to 1917.[27]

Business enterprises were not considered outside of the realm of womanly activity. An interesting example of success in this area appears in an 1881 sketch of the life of Eliza R. Snow:

> Sister Eliza entered upon her duties as superintendent of the Woman's Store immediately after the October Conference, 1876, and by her careful and prudent management and her practical executive ability, succeeded in establishing without money a home manufacture mercantile department, which still exists as proof positive of her eminent success in this line of labor. President Young fully acknowledged she had done what he had been trying for years to get one or more of the brethren to do, but could not persuade them to undertake it without capital. Sister Eliza thus demonstrated the fact that women have faith and courage to undertake what men would consider a hopeless enterprise. Goods were sold on commission, lady clerks were employed, and a lady sat at the desk and kept the books. Sister Eliza not only looked after the minutest details of work, but actually performed some of the real labor herself.[28]

A variety of other skills were also being developed by the women of the Utah territory. In 1872 the *Exponent* boasted that "today on the thousand miles of telegraph lines owned and worked in Utah, the Deseret Telegraph Company employs more lady operators than can be found on the same distance of wire in any other part of the world."[29]

Throughout the pages of their publications, the Mormon women noted their sisters' achievements in all fields — Emma Lucy Gates's outstanding public appearance after returning

---

[27]Susa Young Gates, *Women of the 'Mormon' Church* (n. p., n. d.), p. 25.
[28]"Pen Sketch of an Illustrious Woman," *Woman's Exponent,* 10 (August 15, 1881), 43.
[29]"Lady Lawyers," p. 68.

from a three years' course of music study in Germany[30]; new inventions such as a "dress fitting model that is likely to revolutionize the dress cutting systems of the world," developed by Dora Bigelow of Provo,[31] and a speedometer to be placed on the exterior of automobiles, developed by Mrs. J. F. Gardner of Salt Lake City.[32]

But it was not only their own sisters in the Rocky Mountains whose advances in professional areas the Mormon women followed with interest. The pages of their periodicals document activities of women across the nation — a woman editor of a new periodical published in Washington, the youngest official in the post office department (a fourteen-year-old postmistress in Alaska), the first graduate of the Army School of Nursing to be appointed in the Army Nurse Corps, the first woman to be chief executive of a major opera company, women serving successfully as fire lookouts in Oregon, a woman master machinist (the first woman honored to be elected to the American Society of Mechanical Engineers, "a very attractive, womanly woman, in no way mannish").[33]

The challenge left by these incredible women, who pioneered not only the land, but social and professional frontiers as well, is aptly put by Church Historian Leonard J. Arrington:

> Having made positive contributions in economics and business, in literature, in the professions, and in politics, the Latter-day Saint women set a record of which the area can be proud. Moreover, the Mormon tradition of womanly independence and distinction should inspire a later generation of women who are seeking their rightful place in the world. Our pioneer women's success in combining Church service, professional achievement, and family life, while somewhat intimidating, should awaken modern Latter-day Saint women to their own opportunities and responsibilities.[34]

---

[30]*Young Woman's Journal,* 13 (January 1902), 43.

[31]"A Useful Invention," *Young Woman's Journal,* 13 (April 1902), 187.

[32]*Relief Society Magazine,* 9 (January 1922), 46.

[33]"In the Realm of Women," *Young Woman's Journal,* 32 (August 1921), 489.

[34]Arrington, "Blessed Damozels: Women In Mormon History," p. 31.

Again, we must be aware that these women were not advocating professional careers in place of the establishment of a home and the rearing of children. But knowing that not all women married, that not all married women were fully occupied with home and children for the entirety of their lives, that wives and mothers were more capable if they had received some sort of specialized training and experience, and that many women had particular gifts that if given would better the world — knowing these things, the early Mormon women devoted themselves to preparing for and making significant contributions. Perhaps many of them heard and remembered those wise words of Eliza as she was issuing the call to become doctors of medicine:

> Let your first business be to perform your duties at home. But inasmuch as you are wise stewards, . . . you will find that your capacity will increase, and you will be astonished at what you can accomplish. . . . God bless you, my sisters, and encourage you, that you may be filled with light.[35]

---

[35]Eliza R. Snow, "Address," p. 37.

CHAPTER 9

One More Voice:
A Personal Perspective

Dear Emily and Katharine,

(True, Katharine has not arrived yet. In fact, there's no way to ascertain that it is a girl who has been tapping away on the inside while I have been typing away on the outside. But we're planning on a girl, and have requested one. After all, there must be some left over from those dark days when people prayed only for a man-child. Not that we wouldn't welcome a third boy — Johnny and Aaron are such terrific little people — but this is a good day for women, and so we're hoping for another.)

I have chosen, my girls, to write this last chapter as a personal message to you. And if others wish to join us, I welcome them. I am hopeful that you respect the words, the experiences of our foremothers as I do, that you have learned something from them, and that you will not let their documents be destroyed. (Yes, Emily, especially that muslin-bound volume of 1880 *Exponents* you spilled Kool-Aid on while helping me write this book by pressing the return button on the typewriter each time I said "now.") Those good women have left you valuable observations. May I attempt a few of my own?

From the days of the first woman's rights convention in Seneca Falls in 1848, enormous change has occurred in

Mary Cooper Oakey

Emily Pearson

Sarah Oakey Sirrine

Carol Lynn Wright Pearson

Emeline Sirrine Wright

the lives and the position of women. I am aware of people who believe the change has all been for the worse, that we would all be better off in the good old days when women knew their place and stayed in it. I don't believe that. I believe that today is the good day for women — and for men as well, for in the words of Alfred, Lord Tennyson, "The woman's cause is man's — they rise or sink together." Today, even with all its dangers, its confusions, its counterfeits, is the good day for women. It is not easy to look back and to look around and determine what is progress and what is not, what is good and what is bad, in regard to the multifaceted "woman question." It seems to me that we might look at it in terms of a statement made by Brigham Young. He said, "I call evil inverted truth, or a correct principle made an evil use of." I am convinced that the "correct principle" in this case is that really revolutionary idea, quite new to human thought, that to be a woman is as big a prize as to be a man. And the "evil uses of" this principle certainly exist today, in both manifest and subtle forms.

Now, why this whole problem had to be in the first place, I don't know. It had something to do with the fall of our first parents, perhaps, but just what I am not sure and I don't know of anyone who is. I don't know why Gallup polls of my generation show that approximately one-third of the female populace would prefer to be born men if they could choose (while 4 percent of men would choose to be women). I don't know why — when a woman of my acquaintance, confused and unable to find answers to important questions, asked her husband in dismay, "What would you do if you had been born a woman?" — why his reply was, "Well, I guess I'd just make the best of a bad deal." Why these things have to be in the first place, I don't know. But I know that they are. I also know that they're being challenged, which delights me. But the challenge presents many possibilities for destructive choices, which frightens me.

I will try to present some observations about all this in terms of the title I chose for this book, *The Flight and the Nest*. It appears to me that the greatest danger we have to face, and that perhaps you will have to face, is an under-evaluation of the nest. And certainly the most wonderful thing about all that has happened for woman is the opening of the world for her flight. Somehow — and certainly it will be in a different way and in a different time for each — a woman must strike some harmonious balance between the flight and the nest in her life.

I can add my witness to those that have been borne in this book by our foremothers that the business of supreme value in this world is the creation of human beings, and through them the creation of a society that is the sort our Heavenly Parents would wish for their children to live in. Somehow they designed marriage and parenthood as basic to all this, essential for the growth of the parent and for the growth of the child. These relationships, I have dis-covered, are designed to develop in human beings qualities of character that do not come so quickly, or in quite the same way, from other avenues. A statement I have quoted often is from one of the apostles of my generation, Elder Boyd K. Packer: "In no other way can man or woman become as God quite so quickly as in family living."

I feel that one of the least exposed truths in the litera-ture of my day is that motherhood is about the greatest "liberation" that can come to a woman (or fatherhood to a man, if he will take it seriously). It is, of course, confining in some rather obvious ways (the heaviness, the bearing, the healing, the nursing), but you will learn as I have that the physical dimensions of practically anything are the least significant ones. And in the case of motherhood the doors that open are more numerous and more important than those that close.

For each woman the openings would be somewhat dif-ferent. I will try to describe what to me was one of the most significant. When my first child arrived seven years ago this weekend (yes, Emily, it was you), I found that I had an opportunity to begin my life all over again. Not by living it through you — that would only damage both of us. But suddenly, for the first time in my adult life, I could begin a relationship that was not inhibited by adult expectations and by established self-images. You did not know my inadequacies. You did not know that I did not consider myself the attractive, warm, giving, socially competent person that I would like to be. You accepted me as everything good and loved me without qualification. And things began growing in me that were rather new. I began to see myself becoming more of the person I wanted to be. Did you demand it? invite it? permit it? I don't know. But it has continued with your brothers, and I thank you all.

As for the importance of these nest relationships to the children — it should be evident. An anthropologist of whom I am fond, Ashley Montague, put it this way: "For it is in the home that human beings are formed, and it is human beings who mold the world according to the kingdom that is within them." Will you keep that thought in the back of your mind while I tell you a little story?

When your father and I took you, Emily, to London, when you were less than a year old (we had saved up to get a taste of British theatre, both of us having graduated from BYU in drama), you and I would often go out in the stroller (you in it, me pushing it). A lovely place was just a few blocks from our flat — Kensington Gardens (yes, that's where Peter Pan ran away from). There was a lovely little lake there, and one day as we sat beside it I began conversing with an old man who was sitting on the same bench. He told me how things were there during the war, how when it was foggy people would sneak up to the lake and catch the ducks for their supper. He had been a pilot in the war, and prior to that had spent some time in Austria and Germany.

"I knew Hitler's mother," he said.

"You did?" This really blew my mind because I guess it had never occurred to me that Hitler had a mother. "What sort of a person was she?"

"Oh, she was a witch — an absolute witch."

"Really? Tell me about her."

But he didn't want to talk about it. And, much as I tried, I could get nothing more from him. Before long he strolled off. Now, I have not done my homework on this subject, and I probably should not repeat this story without finding out what truth I can about Hitler's mother. But, just on speculation, I began to think about that. What if Hitler's mother were indeed a witch, or at least the sort of human being one would not deliberately choose to give to another human being as a mother? Not that we could then say, "Well, poor little Hitler, he never had a chance." But we would have to expect that when comes whatever final judgment is coming, there would have to be at least one more person, perhaps others, who will have to stand responsible for all that happened to the world because of Hitler. "For it is in the home that human beings are formed, and it is human beings who mold the world according to the kingdom that is within them." Hitler did indeed mold the world, did he not?

With few exceptions a mother is the child's first window into the world. How important that she be the sort of person that can well serve as a model. And how important that she be willing to provide, in both quality and quantity, the emotional and spiritual nourishment that is needed.

Two and a half years ago your father gave me for Christmas a set of eight books on the subject of woman's history and the current woman's movement. (Some men would be appalled at the very thought, but your father is braver than most.) In those books I discovered some stimulating and thrilling things. And I also discovered some rather terrifying things. One such is a statement made in behalf of the need for a massive network of public day-care centers so that women can "conserve their energies for service to humanity." (There are cases in which day-care is necessary and desirable, and the facilities should be better than most are, but the point I'm making concerns the logic of the whole statement.)

"Service to humanity." You see what an amazing pass my generation has come to. Our idea of service and progress has become very warped. We live in a day in which most of the families in America can turn on their television, sit back, and watch — often in color, sometimes live, beamed off a satellite — pictures of people killing one another, committing all kinds of immoral and unethical acts, performing dishonestly in high places. "Service to humanity." We do not need so much the technological advancement of producing a clearer picture as we need to *change* the picture. And we don't need so much an improvement in sound as to change what is being *said*.

Herein appears to me the most dangerous temptation to women. Because the world has always assumed that what men have been involved in is more important than what women have been involved in, we accept it as a fact. And now that we have our freedom (too long in the coming) we are sorely tempted to use it to emulate something not worthy of emulation. Many men have done great and noble things and had their values in the right place. But by and large the power structure has held material values above human values. And inasmuch as Jack might fall down the hill, must Jill go tumbling after? If all women — and men as well — really desire to give service to humanity, they will see what humanity needs most is human beings of the sort that can make the world the place it might be — honest, responsible, loved and loving human beings (firstly yourself, then members of your own family, then whomever else you might influence). And after that job is done (to some extent concurrent with it) any other contributions that can come will be additional and welcome service.

Another misconception that my generation has, and it's related to our technological infatuation, is the notion that he or she who is most economically productive is the most successful. I found a statement some months ago that rang with truth to me. It was attributed to William Jennings Bryan: "The human measure of a human life is its income; the divine measure of a life is its outgo, its overflow — its contribution to the welfare of all." Would it not be an amazing step forward if every human being believed and practiced that? Especially women who for the first time have the option of choosing an income? Not that work by those of our sex shouldn't receive as much remuneration as is given the other; but we must firstly be concerned with our outgo.

That human life which we have come to accept as the ideal for us all — that of Jesus Christ — was not marked by its income. I am not aware that he was paid anything for the mission he fulfilled (perhaps earlier, yes, for carpentry work, but nothing for his teaching and his sacrifice). His life, however, was transcendently successful because of its outgo, because he gave to the world what was within him to give. Within each person, man and woman, are many things to give; our job is to discover, to develop, and to give them. Somewhere along the way enough money must be earned to keep the family reasonably well cared for, and each couple has the right to decide how this can best be done, keeping in mind their family priorities.

To be able, then, to have an "outgo," to make a "contribution to the welfare of all," requires that one not be empty. And here we must consider for a moment the concept of "femininity." There is no way in this world that everyone of my generation and probably of yours could agree on what is properly feminine. And that's fine — we need variety. Such basics as graciousness, warmth, charm, beauty (not necessarily the contest kind) are always to be sought for, I believe. But hopefully we are getting away from some of the damaging qualities that are currently part of the package being sold by many people. As dangerous as the radicals on the one hand who would emulate all that men have traditionally been are those on the other extreme who would have us be as unlike men as possible. This philosophy urges that we be weak, fearful, incapable of serious thinking, unable to make a weighty decision, nonachievers in anything but the domestic, self-demeaning, unoriginal, and highly dependent. This philosophy promises that by developing these traits we can add much to the happiness of our marriage and our homes. May I suggest that it can, perhaps, solve some problems temporarily, but that it ignores the absolute necessity of growth, both in the person and in the relationship. When we deliberately deny some basic human needs in the name of femininity, when we mold ourselves to a pattern smaller than our own souls, we are doing great damage indeed. Of course we hurt ourselves, sometimes in ways that might not surface for years and years. And then, as important as marriage is, to deliberately present the men we love with companions who are empty and stunted — what an incredible disservice to them! There are those, yes, who require that someone else be less in order that they can be more, but I believe that in general our men are coming around to the realization that it is no fun to be unevenly yoked, in mind, in spirit, in interests. And, as absolutely vital as is the office of motherhood, to present to our children mothers who are less than they might be — what an unforgivable damage to them! To have children raising other children is perhaps as wise as to have the blind leading the blind.

My counsel, then, is not to fear development, not to shun excellence. If you will couple your excellence with humility, no one can be damaged, and everyone can be made richer. I have no quarrel with the statement that "the woman's place is in the home," as long as we punctuate it reasonably. I would end it with a semicolon and add something like, "and when the home is in good order and priorities well placed, then in due time and with good sense and good cooperation and support from husband and children, she can extend herself into any arena of activity that registers righteously within her."

I would not have you think, however, that your excellence must be necessarily public — that in addition to creating a family you must one day write a book, become a medical doctor, serve on the Supreme Court. Do not rule these out if the seeds of these contributions are within you and call to be cultivated. (Some people call going into these areas competition; I call it contribution.) But do not look down upon yourself or upon other women if the achievements that emerge are not highly visible. A woman can, without much public contact, without salary, without awards, make significant progress in her own development and in the development of others.

Finally, a few words about status. Why our judgments in this world must so often be vertical, I don't know. But they are. We have totem poles, and somehow femaleness has been carved almost universally below maleness. You probably have met and likely will meet this attitude in many forms. (Such as is betrayed in the comment of my friend's husband early in their marriage: "Look, don't ever ask me to change a diaper — that is squaw work, and I will have none of it." As if driving a truck for Coca Cola is more eternally significant than the direct nurturance of a human being. How many men have lost out on the better things under the illusion of getting away with something.) The Lord has told us that the last shall be first and the first shall be last. I don't take that to mean that our totems will be turned upside down for the eternities, but that somehow we are incredibly fouled up in the way we have made assignments of status, and that one day we will have some enormous surprises.

Men have, you know, been called upon by tradition to do as much damage to their souls in the name of a strange "masculinity" as women have sometimes done in the name of a false "femininity." Remember the characteristics that "Santiago" assigned to man in that intriguing exchange in the *Young Woman's Journal?* He was "strong, forceful, stern, merciless, imperious, striding over all opposition." And woman was "gentle, kind, loving, forgiving, full of mercy and charity."

Which of these lists sounds as if it were drawn up by Christ? Which, in fact, are those very virtues that we are explicitly told the exercise of a man's priesthood is based upon? There will always be, I think, wonderful differences between man and woman, but as we get rid of some of the false notions we can develop men and women that are more civilized, men and women that are closer to the example of Christ.

Another statement made by our Lord is absolutely central to what we're talking about. The apostles, you may remember, at the time of the Last Supper, were strangely involved. As related in three of the Gospels, they were quarreling among themselves as to who should be accounted the greatest. (See? It's gone on for centuries, this masculine endorsement of competitive aggression, this compulsion to be "top dog".) But that was not what Christ wished to teach his disciples, nor do I expect it's what he would have any of us learn today. His words and his actions on that occasion are profound, and led me to write the following poem:

HE WHO WOULD BE CHIEF AMONG YOU

And he rose from supper,
Poured water in a basin,
And washed the disciples' feet.

Those hands,
Hardened by the heat of a desert sun,
Comfortable with cutting trees
And turning them to tables
In Joseph's shop —

Those hands,
That with a wave could stop
The troubled sea,
Could touch a leper clean,
Or triumphantly turn death away
From the loved daughter on Jairus' couch —

Those hands,
That could gesture the heavens open —
Poured water in a basin
And washed the disciples' feet.

The lesson lies unlearned
But to a few,
Who trust the paradox
And hear the call:

"He who would be chief among you,
Let him be the servant of all."

If, then, we are to take the Lord at his word, the greatest ambition of any of us, man or woman, would be to become a servant. Not that we would therefore ask nothing for ourselves. But that we would therefore ask for ourselves every-thing — everything that would make us the most effective servant we might possibly be, on whatever level of human endeavor we might find ourselves, at home or elsewhere.

Before you establish your own nests, devote yourselves to the flight. If for some reason the nest should not be part of your destiny, you will then be prepared to live a life that still is filled with satisfaction and productivity. And if you do find your own nests, and I hope that you will, the place and the people will be richer for all you can give them.

I have thought a great deal about the women of my past and the women of my future. I look forward to the day that we will all be together in that more permanent place — Mary, Sarah, Emeline, Carol Lynn, Emily, Katharine, and all the other women and men that form the links of family and friendship. We'll know a lot more then about womanhood and manhood, as well as about other vital subjects. In the meantime, let us devote ourselves as best we can to the learn-ing, and to the doing.

Love from your mother,

Carol Lynn

Index

God, 14
Government, 79
Grant, Heber J., remarks at funeral
of Emily S. Tanner Richards, 40
Greece, women's movement in, 4
Greene, Louisa Lulu, *See* Richards,
Louisa Lulu Greene
Greenwood, Grace, on womanhood, 42
Grover, Hannah, on effect of pioneer-
ing on women, 45-46
"Growing Old" (*Woman's Exponent*),
91-92

- H -

Hart, Lalene H., on woman's responsi-
bilities, 82
Harvard College, 66-67
"He Who Would Be Chief Among You"
(Pearson), 112
Higginson, Colonel, on work of a wife,
89
Hill, Flora S., on woman's purpose, 18-19
History of Relief Society 1842-1966, 8
"History of the Emancipation of Wo-
men (Singer), 6
*History of the Young Ladies Mutual
Improvement Association* (Gates),
16
History, of woman's progress, 4-5
Hitler, 106-107
mother of, 106-107
Hodapp, Minnie I., on Susan B.
Anthony, 34-35
Home, 55
duties, 101
reaching out from, 8
true, 54
"Home Companionship" (*Young Wo-
man's Journal*), 39
"Home Influence" (Camelia), 55
Homemaker, position of, 87
Howard, Mary, woman mayor, 82
Howe, Julia Ward, 37, 70
Human beings, creation of, 105
Humanity, greatest need of, 108
love of, 20
service to, 107-108
Humility, 110

- I -

Ignorance, 64, 68
"Impulse of the Hour, The" (Hill),
18-19

Integrity, 20
Intelligence, standards of, 45
Inventions, developed by women, 100
Isabella of Castille, 6
Israel, mother in, 59-60
Italy, woman's emergence in, 4, 5

- J -

Jesus Christ, 5, 109, 112
teachings of, 60
Jordan, 43

- K -

Kelsey, Valeria DeMude, "Vision or
Dream," 50
Kensington Gardens, 106
"Key Turned for Women, The" (*Relief
Society Magazine*), 7, 9
Kimball, Sarah M., 27
King, Hannah T., 98
Knowledge, 20, 63, 64

- L -

"Lady Lawyers" (*Woman's Exponent*),
95
Last Supper, apostles at, 112
Learning, women's quest for, 6
Legislation, permitting women to vote,
71
"Liberation," greatest, 105
Liberty, 20
"Life and Work of Susan B. Anthony,
The" (*Young Woman's Journal*),
31-33
*Lighter of Lamps, The Life Story of
Alice Louise Reynolds, A* (Lyman),
72
Literature, Mormon women in field of,
98
Lockwood, Belva A., 84
Love, 49
Luther, Martin, 5
Lyman, Amy Brown, 72
on women in government, 83

- M -

"Maid and Her Admirers, The" (Peay),
90-91
Man, woman's equality with, 26
Mann, Horace, 54

120 *Index*

- T -

"Taking a Stand for the Right" (Peay), 14
Tanner, Mary J., 98
Tanner, N. Eldon, on Utah women in public service, 80
Taylor, John W., on Eliza R. Snow, 59-60
"Teacher of Girls, The" (Nuttall), 67-68
Tennyson, Alfred, Lord, on woman's cause, 104
"Ten Years of Suffrage" (*Relief Society Magazine*), 75
Tingey, Mattie Horne, on woman's individuality, 43-44
"To Your Task, O Women!" (Fox), 58, 61
Training, mental, 64
"Treasurers" (Higginson), 89
Tremain, Rose, on tyranny over women, 36
Trust, 30
Tullidge, Edward W., on Relief Society, 72

- U -

"Union Forever" (Gates), 15
Unity, in marriage, 43
Universities, closed to women, 5
University of Bologna, 5
University of Utah, 67
"Useful Invention, A" (*Young Woman's Journal*), 100
Utah, 95
  first election to the State Senate in, 80
  state constitution of, 79
  women in, 94
Utah Woman Suffrage Song Book, 73-74

- V -

"Valedictory" (Richards), 51
Victoria, Queen, 84
Views, extreme, 15
"Vision or Dream" (Kelsey), 50
Vocations, every girl to qualify in two, 90
  women prepared to fill, 91

- W -

Washington, George, 59
Weed, Thomas, 32

Wells, Emmeline B., 75, 76
  on idea of a woman president, 84
  on redemption of women, 12
  on Susan B. Anthony, 31-33
  on woman's awakening, 16-17
  on woman's part, 25
  on woman's progress as an individual, 44
  on women authors and journalists, 98
"What Men Admire in Women" (*Young Woman's Journal*), 40
"What Pioneering Does for Womanhood" (Grover), 45-46
Whitney, Orson F., on Mother in Heaven, 10-11
"Who's Afraid of Women Priests?" (Boyd), 9
Widtsoe, John A., 86
Widtsoe, Leah D., on motherhood, 56, 60
Wife, work of, 87-89
Wives, support of, 87-89
Woman, admirable, 40
  aspirations of, for equality, 17-18
  childless, 60
  co-equal with man, 14
  created for noble purpose, 18
  essay on, 4-6
  greatest service of, 52
  prospect of the average 40-year-old, 91-92
  rebellion of, 4
  redemption of, 12
  rights of, 14
  sphere of, 92-93
  three ways of looking at, 43
  true, 18-19
  unmarried, 90
  what it means to be a, 45-46
"Woman and Her Duties" (*Woman's Exponent*), 58
"Woman Arise!" (Dalton), 24
"Woman, Arise" (Richards), 73-74
Womanhood, 45
  new concept of, 42
"Woman in Politics" (L.E.H.), 78-79
"Woman's Bill," 76
Woman's Exponent, 1, 17, 27, 71, 96
  first editor of, 51
  ideas exchanged in, 62
"Woman's Idea, The" (*Relief Society Magazine*), 82-83
"Woman's Influence" (*Young Woman's Journal*), 52
"Woman's Position" (Crosby), 63